interactive SCIENCE

A porcupine's hollow quills help it stay afloat while swimming.

PEARSON

Glenview, Illinois • Boston, Massachusetts • Chandler, Arizona • Upper Saddle River, New Jersey

Authors

You are an author!

This is your own special book to keep. You can write all of your science discoveries in your book. That is why you are an author of this book.

Print your name, school, town, and state below. Then write to tell everyone all about you.

My Picture

Name

School

Town

State

All About Me

Credits appear on pages EM36–EM38, which constitute an extension of this copyright page.

PEARSON

ISBN-13: 978-0-328-52097-8
ISBN-10: 0-328-52097-7
21 20

On The Cover
The porcupine's hollow quills help it stay afloat while swimming.

Program Authors

DON BUCKLEY, M.Sc.
*Information and Communications Technology Director,
The School at Columbia University, New York, New York*
Mr. Buckley has been at the forefront of K–12 educational
technology for nearly two decades. A founder of New York City
Independent School Technologists (NYCIST) and long-time chair
of New York Association of Independent Schools' annual IT
conference, he has taught students on two continents and
created multimedia and Internet-based instructional systems
for schools worldwide.

ZIPPORAH MILLER, M.A.Ed.
*Associate Executive Director for Professional Programs
and Conferences, National Science Teachers Association,
Arlington, Virginia*
Associate executive director for professional programs and
conferences at NSTA, Ms. Zipporah Miller is a former K–12 science
supervisor and STEM coordinator for the Prince George's County
Public School District in Maryland. She is a science education
consultant who has overseen curriculum development and staff
training for more than 150 district science coordinators.

MICHAEL J. PADILLA, Ph.D.
*Associate Dean and Director, Eugene P. Moore School of
Education, Clemson University, Clemson, South Carolina*
A former middle school teacher and a leader in middle school science
education, Dr. Michael Padilla has served as president of the National
Science Teachers Association and as a writer of the National Science
Education Standards. He is professor of science education at Clemson
University. As lead author of the *Science Explorer* series, Dr. Padilla
has inspired the team in developing a program that promotes student
inquiry and meets the needs of today's students.

KATHRYN THORNTON, Ph.D.
*Professor and Associate Dean, School of Engineering
and Applied Science, University of Virginia,
Charlottesville, Virginia*
Selected by NASA in May 1984, Dr. Kathryn Thornton is a veteran
of four space flights. She has logged over 975 hours in space,
including more than 21 hours of extravehicular activity. As an
author on the *Scott Foresman Science* series, Dr. Thornton's
enthusiasm for science has inspired teachers around the globe.

MICHAEL E. WYSESSION, Ph.D.
*Associate Professor of Earth and Planetary Science,
Washington University, St. Louis, Missouri*
An author on more than 50 scientific publications, Dr. Wysession
was awarded the prestigious Packard Foundation Fellowship and
Presidential Faculty Fellowship for his research in geophysics. Dr.
Wysession is an expert on Earth's inner structure and has mapped
various regions of Earth using seismic tomography. He is known
internationally for his work in geoscience education and outreach.

Instructional Design Author

GRANT WIGGINS, Ed.D.
*President, Authentic Education,
Hopewell, New Jersey*
Dr. Wiggins is a co-author with Jay McTighe
of *Understanding by Design, 2nd Edition*
(ASCD 2005). His approach to instructional
design provides teachers with a disciplined
way of thinking about curriculum design,
assessment, and instruction that moves
teaching from covering content to ensuring
understanding.
UNDERSTANDING BY DESIGN® and
UbD® are trademarks of ASCD, and are
used under license.

Planet Diary Author

JACK HANKIN
*Science/Mathematics Teacher,
The Hilldale School, Daly City, California
Founder, Planet Diary Web site*
Mr. Hankin is the creator and writer
of Planet Diary, a science current events
website. Mr. Hankin is passionate about
bringing science news and environmental
awareness into classrooms.

Activities Author

KAREN L. OSTLUND, Ph.D.
*Advisory Council, Texas Natural Science
Center, College of Natural Sciences,
The University of Texas at Austin*
Dr. Ostlund has over 35 years of experience
teaching at elementary, middle school,
and university levels. She was Director of
WINGS Online (Welcoming Interns and
Novices with Guidance and Support) and
Director of the UTeach | Dell Center for New
Teacher Success at the University of Texas at
Austin. She served as Director of the Center
for Science Education at the University of
Texas at Arlington, President of the Council
of Elementary Science International, and
on the Board of Directors of the National
Science Teachers Association. As an author
of *Scott Foresman Science*, Dr. Ostlund was
instrumental in developing inquiry activities.

ELL Consultant

JIM CUMMINS, Ph.D.
*Professor and Canada Research Chair,
Curriculum, Teaching and Learning
Department at the University of Toronto*
Dr. Cummins focuses on literacy development
in multilingual schools and the role of
technology in learning. *Interactive Science*
incorporates research-based principles for
integrating language with the teaching of
academic content based on his work.

Reviewers

Program Consultants

William Brozo, Ph.D.
Professor of Literacy, Graduate School of Education, George Mason University, Fairfax, Virginia.
Dr. Brozo is the author of numerous articles and books on literacy development. He co-authors a column in The Reading Teacher and serves on the editorial review board of the Journal of Adolescent & Adult Literacy.

Kristi Zenchak, M.S.
Biology Instructor, Oakton Community College, Des Plaines, Illinois
Kristi Zenchak helps elementary teachers incorporate science, technology, engineering, and math activities into the classroom. STEM activities that produce viable solutions to real-world problems not only motivate students but also prepare students for future STEM careers. Ms. Zenchak helps elementary teachers understand the basic science concepts, and provides STEM activities that easy are to implement in the classroom.

Content Reviewers

Brad Armosky, M.S.
Texas Advanced Computing Center
University of Texas at Austin
Austin, Texas

Alexander Brands, Ph.D.
Department of Biological Sciences
Lehigh University
Bethlehem, Pennsylvania

Paul Beale, Ph.D.
Department of Physics
University of Colorado
Boulder, Colorado

Joy Branlund, Ph.D.
Department of Earth Science
Southwestern Illinois College
Granite City, Illinois

Constance Brown, Ph.D
Atmospheric Science Program
Geography Department
Indiana University
Bloomington, Indiana

Dana Dudle, Ph.D.
Biology Department
DePauw University
Greencastle, Indiana

Rick Duhrkopf, Ph. D.
Department of Biology
Baylor University
Waco, Texas

Mark Henriksen, Ph.D.
Physics Department
University of Maryland
Baltimore, Maryland

Andrew Hirsch, Ph.D.
Department of Physics
Purdue University
W. Lafayette, Indiana

Linda L. Cronin Jones, Ph.D.
School of Teaching & Learning
University of Florida
Gainesville, Florida

T. Griffith Jones, Ph.D.
College of Education
University of Florida
Gainesville, Florida

Candace Lutzow-Felling, Ph.D.
Director of Education
State Arboretum of Virginia &
Blandy Experimental Farm
Boyce, Virginia

Cortney V. Martin, Ph.D.
Virginia Polytechnic Institute
Blacksburg, Virginia

Sadredin Moosavi, Ph.D.
University of Massachusetts
Dartmouth
Fairhaven, Massachusetts

Klaus Newmann, Ph.D.
Department of Geological Sciences
Ball State University
Muncie, Indiana

Scott M. Rochette, Ph.D.
Department of the Earth Sciences
SUNY College at Brockport
Brockport, New York

Ursula Rosauer Smedly, M.S.
Alcade Science Center
New Mexico State University
Alcade, New Mexico

Frederick W. Taylor, Ph.D.
Jackson School of Geosciences
University of Texas at Austin
Austin, Texas

K-8 National Master Teacher Board

Chapter 1

The Nature of Science

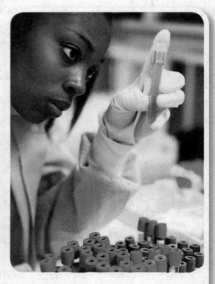

Scientists draw conclusions about the things they study.

myscienceonline.com

Untamed Science
Watch the Ecogeeks as they learn about the nature of science.

Got it? **60-Second Video**
Watch and learn about the nature of science.

Envision It!
See what you already know about the nature of science.

Science Songs
Sing about the nature of science.

? **I Will Know...**
See how the key concepts of the nature of science come to life.

Trains help many people travel long distances.

myscienceonline.com

Untamed Science
Ecogeeks answer your questions about technology and tools.

Got it? 60-Second Video
Review lessons about technology and tools in 60 seconds!

Science Songs
Listen to a catchy tune about technology and tools!

MY PLANET DIARY
Discovery! Find out about a new kind of train in My Planet Diary.

Investigate It! Simulation
Investigate how a machine can ring a bell in this online lab.

Unit B
Life Science

Chapter 3

Plants and Animals

These fish get what they need in the coral reef.

myscienceonline.com

Untamed Science
Watch the Ecogeeks learn about plants and animals.

Got it? 60-Second Video
Take one minute to learn about plants and animals.

Envision It!
See what you already know about plants and animals.

Science Songs
Listen to a catchy tune about plants and animals!

Explore It! Animation
Quick and easy experiments about plants and animals.

Monarch butterflies go through a life cycle.

myscienceonline.com

Untamed Science
Ecogeeks answer your questions about growing and changing.

Got it? 60-Second Video
Review lessons about growing and changing in 60 seconds!

Science Songs
Listen to a catchy tune about growing and changing!

MY PLANET DIARY
Did you know? Learn about zebra longwing butterflies.

Investigate It! Simulation
Investigate the life cycle of a beetle in this online lab.

Earth's Materials

Plants, water, and rocks are natural resources.

mYscienceonLine.com

UntamedScience
Ecogeeks answer your questions about Earth's materials.

Got it? 60-Second Video
Review lessons about Earth's materials in 60 seconds!

MY PLANET DIARY
Did you know? Discover interesting facts about Earth's materials.

Science Songs
Listen to a catchy tune about Earth's materials!

Investigate It! Simulation
Investigate how polluted water can be cleaned in this online lab.

Chapter 6

The Solar System

Plants need sunlight to grow.

myscienceonline.com

Untamed Science
Ecogeeks answer your
questions about the
solar system.

Got it? 60-Second Video
Review lessons about the
solar system in 60 seconds!

MY PLANET DIARY
Did you know? Learn
about the history of the
solar system.

Envision It!
See what you already know
about the solar system.

Vocabulary Smart Cards
Mix and match solar system
vocabulary online.

Chapter 7

Weather

*Scientists measure weather to
warn people about storms.*

myscienceonline.com

Untamed Science
Go on an Ecogeek adventure
to learn about weather.

Got it? 60-Second Video
Take one minute to learn
about weather.

MY PLANET DIARY
Did you know? Learn about
the water cycle.

Envision It!
See what you already know
about weather.

Investigate It! Simulation
Investigate what your
weather is like in this
online lab.

Unit D
Physical Science

Chapter 8

Matter

The bubbles in the picture are filled with gas.

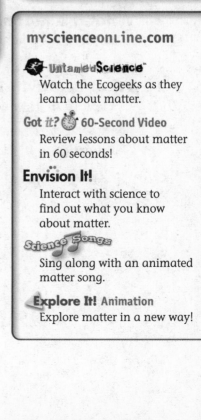

myscienceonline.com

Untamed Science
Watch the Ecogeeks as they learn about matter.

Got it? ⏱ **60-Second Video**
Review lessons about matter in 60 seconds!

Envision It!
Interact with science to find out what you know about matter.

Science Songs
Sing along with an animated matter song.

Explore It! Animation
Explore matter in a new way!

Chapter 9

Energy, Motion, and Force

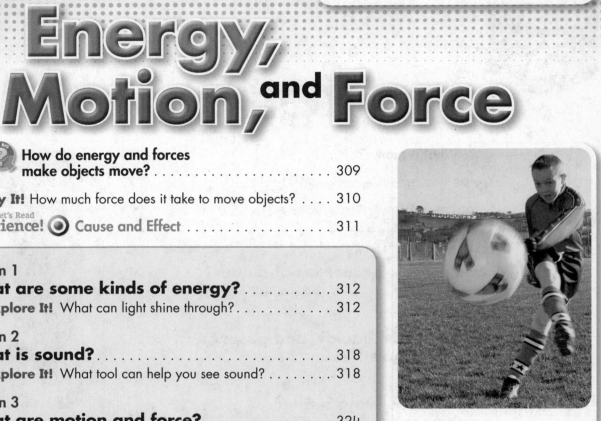

A kick will make a soccer ball move.

myscienceonline.com

Untamed Science
Ecogeeks answer your
questions about energy,
motion, and force.

Got it? 60-Second Video
Review lessons about energy,
motion, and force in
60 seconds!

Envision It!
See what you already know
about energy, motion,
and force.

Explore It! Animation
Watch this energy, motion,
and force experiment online!

Vocabulary Smart Cards
Mix and match energy,
motion, and force
vocabulary.

Untamed Science™

Videos that bring Science to life!

Go to **MyScienceOnline.com** to watch exciting Untamed Science videos!

The Untamed Science team has created a unique video for every chapter in this book!

"This is your book. You can write in it!"

interactive SCIENCE

 Big Question

At the start of each chapter you will see two questions—an **Engaging Question** and a **Big Question.** Just like a scientist, you will predict an answer to the Engaging Question. Each Big Question will help you start thinking about the Big Ideas of science. Look for the symbol throughout the chapter!

How is a young orangutan like its mother?

Plants and Animals

Chapter 4

Try It! How are flowers alike and different?

Lesson 1 What are some groups of living things?

Lesson 2 What are some parts of plants?

Lesson 3 How do plants grow?

Lesson 4 How do some animals grow?

Lesson 5 How are living things like their parents?

Lesson 6 How are groups of living things different?

Investigate It! How do different seeds grow?

Tell one way the baby and its mother are alike.

How are living things alike and different?

Go to www.myscienceonline.com and click on:

InteractiveScience
Ecogeeks answer your questions.

Got it? 60-Second Video
Lesson reviewed in a minute!

112

113

Let's Read Science!

You will see a page like this toward the beginning of each chapter. It will show you how to use a reading skill that will help you understand what you read.

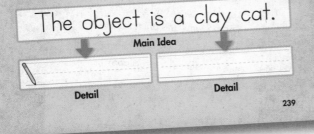

A Clay Cat
The object is a clay cat.
The ears are blue triangles.
The whiskers are long and yellow.

Let's Read Science!

⊙ **Main Idea and Details**
The **main idea** is what the sentences are about.
Details tell about the main idea.

Practice It!
Write two details that tell about the main idea.

The object is a clay cat.

Main Idea

| Detail | Detail |

239

Vocabulary Smart Cards

technology
natural
goal
solution
label

Play a Game!
Cut out the cards.
Work with a partner.
Pick a card.
Show your partner the front of the card.
Have your partner tell what the word means.

solution — solución
technology — tecnología
label — etiqueta
natural — natural
goal — objetivo

59 ✂

Vocabulary Smart Cards

Go to the end of the chapter and cut out your own set of **Vocabulary Smart Cards.** Draw a picture to learn the word. Play a game with a classmate to practice using the word!

Look for **MyScienceOnline.com** technology options.
At MyScienceOnline.com you can immerse yourself in virtual environments, get extra practice, and even blog about current events in science.

"Engage with the page!"

Envision It!

At the beginning of each lesson, at the top of the page, you will see an **Envision It!** interactivity that gives you the opportunity to circle, draw, write, or respond to the Envision It! question.

Lesson 3

How do plants and animals live in land environments?

Envision It!

Tell about where the horses live.

UNLOCK
? I will know how some plants and animals can live in land environments.

Words to Know
environment   prairie
forest   desert

MY PLANET DIARY Did You Know?

Read Together

Look at the bighorn sheep. Why do you think the sheep is called a bighorn?

_____

Some bighorn sheep live in deserts. They eat cactus. A cactus has sharp spines! The sheep use their big horns to scrape off the spines.

Why is this a good idea?

_____
_____
_____

Environments

An **environment** is all living and nonliving things in one place.
An environment has food and water.
An environment has air.
Land is one kind of environment.
Land has rocks and soil.
Many plants and animals live on land.

Write two things you think are in the environment of the raccoon.

_____
_____
_____

86
87

MY PLANET DIARY

My Planet Diary interactivities will introduce you to amazing scientists, fun facts, and important discoveries in science. They will also help you to overcome common misconceptions about science concepts.

Read See DO!

After reading small chunks of information, stop to check your understanding. The visuals help teach about what you read. Answer questions, underline text, draw pictures, or label models.

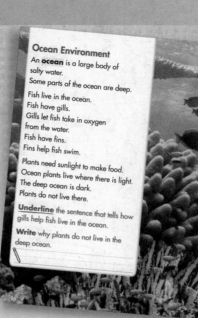

Ocean Environment

An **ocean** is a large body of salty water.
Some parts of the ocean are deep.

Fish live in the ocean.
Fish have gills.
Gills let fish take in oxygen from the water.
Fish have fins.
Fins help fish swim.

Plants need sunlight to make food.
Ocean plants live where there is light.
The deep ocean is dark.
Plants do not live there.

Underline the sentence that tells how gills help fish live in the ocean.

Write why plants do not live in the deep ocean.

Draw an X on the parts of the fish that help it swim.

gills

fins

Do the math! Tally

You can use tally marks to record information.

This is a tally mark. |
These are 5 tally marks. ||||

This chart shows how many trees are in the picture.

Living Things	Tally	Total
Tree			1
Bird		
Lizard		

Write tally marks to record how many birds and lizards are in the picture. Then write the totals.

Find one more living thing in the picture. **Record** the information in the chart.

146

Do the math!

Scientists commonly use math as a tool to help them answer science questions. You can practice skills that you are learning in math class right in your *Interactive Science* Student Edition!

Got it?

At the end of each chapter you will have a chance to evaluate your own progress! At this point you can stop or go on to the next lesson.

Chapter Review — What is Earth made of?

Lesson 1

1. Vocabulary **List** three natural resources.

2. Classify Which natural resource cannot be replaced? **Fill in** the bubble.
   - Ⓐ sunlight
   - Ⓑ air
   - Ⓒ oil
   - Ⓓ water

Lesson 2

3. Main Ideas and Details **Read** the paragraph below. **Underline** two details.
   Diamonds are the hardest minerals on Earth. Diamonds can scratch glass. However, they can be broken with a hammer.

4. Compare **Look** at the rocks. **Write** two ways they are alike.

Lesson 3

5. Identify (Circle) the picture of sandy soil.

Lesson 4

6. Apply **Write** two ways an ocean and a lake are different.

Lesson 5

7. Describe **Write** one way people can protect Earth.

Got it?

🔴 Stop! I need help with

▶ Go! Now I know

202   203

"Have fun! Be a scientist!"

interactive SCIENCE

▲ Try It!

At the start of every chapter, you will have the chance to do a hands-on inquiry activity. The activity will provide you with experiences that will prepare you for the chapter lessons or may raise a new question in your mind.

Inquiry Try It!

What does light do?

☐ 1. Turn on the light.

☐ 2. Shine it at the plastic wrap.
Observe.
Is the light bright?
Is the light dim?
Is there no light?

☐ 3. Repeat with other materials. Record.

Material	Bright Light	Dim Light	No Light

Materials
flashlight
cardboard
white paper
plastic wrap
foil
wax paper

Inquiry Skill
After you observe, you can collect data.

Explain Your Results
4. Observe What did the light do?

270

Lesson 3
What changes land?

Envision It!

before — This volcano erupted.

after — **Tell** how the land changed.

I will know some fast and slow ways Earth changes.

Words to Know
weathering
erosion

Inquiry Explore It!

How does Earth's surface move during an earthquake?

☐ 1. Push the blocks together. Slide them past each other.

☐ 2. Push the blocks together hard. Slide them past each other.

Materials
2 sandpaper blocks

Explain Your Results

3. Did the blocks move smoothly both times? Explain.

4. Infer   An earthquake happens (**fast/slow**). Tell why.

174

Changes on Earth

Earth is always changing. Some changes happen fast. A truck digs a hole in the ground. This is a fast change. Other changes are very slow. A river flows through land. This changes land slowly.

Underline a way Earth can change fast.

This truck moves rocks and soil.

The Colorado River makes the Grand Canyon wider and deeper.

175

▲ Explore It!

Before you start reading the lesson, **Explore It!** activities provide you with an opportunity to first explore the content!

STEM activities are found throughout core and ancillary materials.

Design It!

The **Design It!** activity has you use the engineering design process to find solutions to problems. By finding a problem and then planning, drawing, and choosing materials, you will make, test, and evaluate a solution for a real world problem. Communicate your evidence through drawings and prototypes and identify ways to make your solution better.

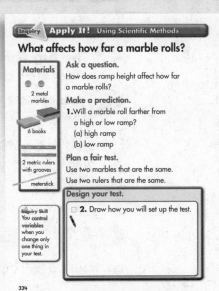

Inquiry **Design It!**

What do pill bugs need?

All pets need habitats. A friend gives you pet pill bugs. You must design a habitat for them. What will your pill bugs need?

Find a problem.

☐ 1. How will you meet each need?

Pill Bug Needs Chart	
Need	How I will meet the need.
Air	
Shelter	
Food (energy)	
Water	

Plan and draw.

☐ 2. List the steps to build the habitat.

☐ 3. Draw your design.
   You will use the materials on the next page.

64   65

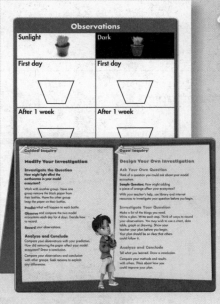

Inquiry **Investigate It!**

Do plants need light?

Follow a Procedure

☐ 1. Water both plants. Draw both plants in the chart.

Materials
2 cups with grass   water

Inquiry Skill You can use a chart to record what you observe.

☐ 2. Put one cup in sunlight. Put one cup in a dark place.

☐ 3. Observe   Check the plants every day. Draw both plants after 1 week.

102

Observations

Sunlight	Dark
First day	First day
After 1 week	After 1 week

Guided Inquiry

Modify Your Investigation

Investigate the Question
How might light affect the earthworms in your model ecosystem?

Work with another group. Have one group remove the black paper from their bottles. Have the other group keep the paper on their bottles.
Predict what will happen to each bottle.
Observe and compare the two model ecosystems each day for 4 days. Decide how to record.
Record your observations.

Analyze and Conclude

Compare your observations with your prediction. How did removing the paper affect your model ecosystem? Draw a conclusion.

Compare your observations and conclusion with other groups. Seek reasons to explain any differences.

Open Inquiry

Design Your Own Investigation

Ask Your Own Question
Think of a question you could ask about your model ecosystem.
Sample Question: How might adding a piece of orange affect your ecosystem?
With your teacher's help, use library and internet resources to investigate your question before you begin.

Investigate Your Question
Make a list of the things you need.
Write a plan. Write each step. Think of ways to record your observations. You may wish to use a chart, data table, graph or drawing. Show your teacher your plan before you begin. Your plan should be so clear that others could follow it.

Analyze and Conclude
Tell what you learned. Draw a conclusion.
Compare your methods and results with others. Think about how you could improve your plan.

Investigate It!

At the end of every chapter, a Directed Inquiry activity gives you a chance to put together everything you've learned in the chapter. Using the activity card, apply design principles in the Guided version to Modify Your Investigation or the Open version to Develop Your Own Investigation. Whether you need a lot of support from your teacher or you're ready to explore on your own, there are fun hands-on activities that match your interests.

Apply It!

At the end of every unit, an Open Inquiry activity gives you a chance to explore science using scientific methods.

Inquiry **Apply It!**   Using Scientific Methods

What affects how far a marble rolls?

Materials
2 metal marbles
6 books
2 metric rulers with grooves
meterstick

Inquiry Skill You control variables when you change only one thing in your test.

Ask a question.
How does ramp height affect how far a marble rolls?

Make a prediction.
1. Will a marble roll farther from a high or low ramp?
   (a) high ramp
   (b) low ramp

Plan a fair test.
Use two marbles that are the same.
Use two rulers that are the same.

Design your test.
☐ 2. Draw how you will set up the test.

☐ 3. Write your steps.

Do your test.
☐ 4. Follow your steps.

Collect and record data.
☐ 5. Fill in the chart.

Tell your conclusion.
6. Communicate   How does ramp height affect how distance rolled?

324   325

"Go online anytime!"

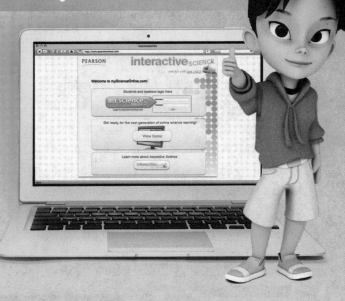

Here's how you log in...

1 Go to www.myscienceonline.com.

2 Log in with your username and password.

Username: _____

Password: _____

3 Click on your program and select your chapter.

Check it out!

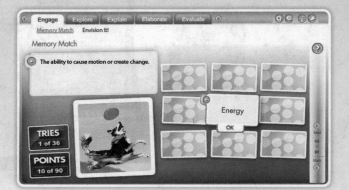

Watch a Video!

 Untamed Science™ Join the Ecogeeks on their video adventure.

Got it? **60-Second Video** Review each lesson in 60 seconds.

Go Digital for Inquiry!

Explore It! Simulation Watch the lab online.

Investigate It! Virtual Lab Do the lab online.

Show What You Know!

Got it? Quiz Take a quick quiz and get instant feedback.

Benchmark Practice Prepare for the "big test."

Writing for Science Write to help you unlock the Big Question.

Get Excited About Science!

The Big Question Share what you think about the Big Question.

my PLANET DIARY Connect to the world of science.

Envision It! Connect to what you already know before you start each lesson.

Memory Match Play a game to build your vocabulary.

Get Help!

MY SCIENCE COACH Get help at your level.

Science, Engineering, and Technology

What does he want to ask?

The Nature of Science

Tell a partner what makes this boy a scientist.

What is science?

Go to www.myscienceonline.com and click on: ⊗

Untamed Science
Watch the Ecogeeks in this wild video.

Got it? 60-Second Video
Review each lesson in 60 seconds!

3

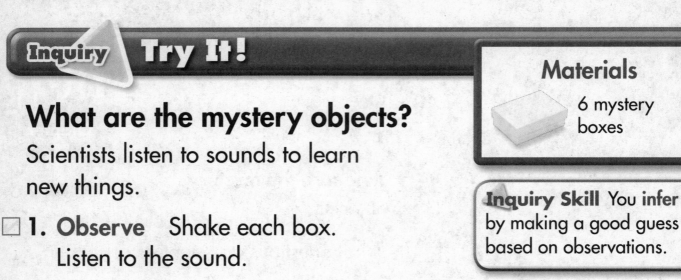

Materials

6 mystery boxes

Inquiry Skill You infer by making a good guess based on observations.

What are the mystery objects?

Scientists listen to sounds to learn new things.

☐ **1. Observe**   Shake each box. Listen to the sound.

☐ **2.** Look at the pictures. What could make each sound?

☐ **3. Infer**   Write the letter of the box by each picture.

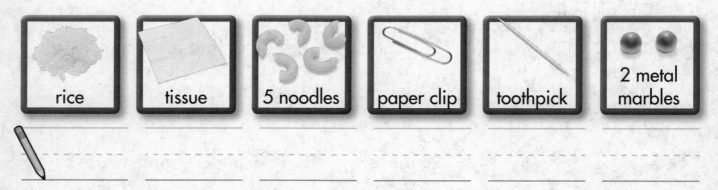

| rice | tissue | 5 noodles | paper clip | toothpick | 2 metal marbles |

☐ **4.** Open each box to find out what is inside.

Explain Your Results

5. Communicate   Think like a scientist. Explain how you decided what was in each box.

Picture Clues

Pictures can give you **clues** about what you read.

Scientists

Scientists use tools to investigate. This girl is a scientist. She measures. She observes. She observes some more. Soon she will learn something new!

Practice It!

Look at the picture. What are two tools that scientists use?

Scientists use tools.

Clue

Clue

What questions do scientists ask?

Envision It!

Tell one question scientists might ask about Mars.

my planet diary

DISCOVERY

Read Together

Lunch is served! This astronaut put water back into her food. She is ready to eat!

Astronauts take food with them when they take off from the Kennedy Space Center in Florida. Scientists found a way to take food into space.

Many foods, like soup and macaroni and cheese, contain water. Scientists take water out of food so the food lasts longer. Astronauts put water back into the food before they eat it.

Tell what else scientists might need in space.

6

Word to Know

inquiry

Scientists

People who study the world around them are scientists. You are a scientist too. Scientists use inquiry to learn. **Inquiry** means asking questions and looking for answers.

This person asks questions about space. He uses a telescope to find answers.

This person is looking for answers to his questions about space.

⊙ **Picture Clues** How is the scientist learning about space? **Look** at the picture. **Write** what you see.

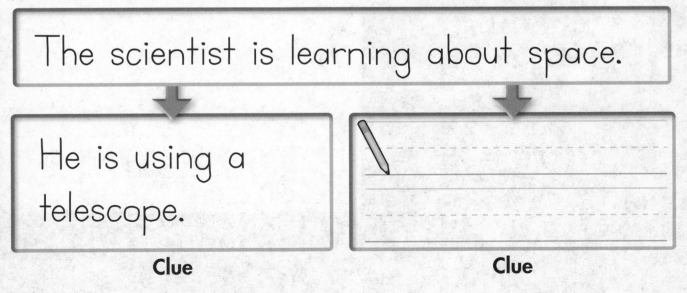

The scientist is learning about space.

He is using a telescope.

Clue

Clue

7

Scientists ask questions about plants.

Questions

Scientists ask questions about the world. Scientists ask questions about plants and animals. They ask questions about rocks and soil. They ask questions about space too. Scientists use inquiry to find answers to their questions.

Scientists know plants need soil to live and grow. They know there is no soil in space. They asked, "How might plants be grown in space without soil?" Then they looked for an answer.

Underline a question that scientists asked.

Write a question you might ask about plants in space.

Discovery

Scientists discovered ways to grow plants without soil. They found out what nutrients plants need from soil. Then they added the nutrients to water. They put the roots of some plants in the water. They observed how the plants grew. Scientists shared what they learned. They explained how plants could grow in space without soil. Now they can grow plants in space.

(Circle) the discovery that scientists made.

Draw an X to show where nutrients were added.

Scientists found an answer to their question. They are growing plants without soil.

These tomatoes were grown without soil.

What kinds of skills do scientists use?

Envision It!

Tell what you could learn about this market by using your senses.

Explore It!

How can you sort objects?

Think about the skills you use as you do this activity.

Materials

paper shapes

☐ 1. **Observe** Work alone. Think of one way to classify the shapes. Sort into groups.

I classified the shapes by _____.

☐ 2. Work with a group. Classify them in another way.

We classified the shapes by _____.

Explain Your Results

3. **Communicate** What skills did you use to sort the shapes?

_____

_____

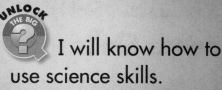

Word to Know

observe

Different Ways to Learn

Scientists learn about the world around them. They find out what they know in many different ways. Scientists use their senses.

Scientists do experiments to learn. They do experiments again and again to make sure they get the same results.

These scientists want to know how tall the plant will grow.

Scientists learn from each other too. They ask each other, "How do you know?" They share what they learn. They give answers. They tell how they know.

Why might scientists want to learn from each other?

_____

_____

_____

_____

11

Science Skills

Observe

Scientists observe to find out about the world. You **observe** when you use your senses to find out about something.

How do you know when an apple is ripe? You might look at the color. Some people tap it to hear how it sounds. You might feel it and smell it too. You will know if it is ripe when you taste it!

Predict

Scientists use what they observe to predict. You predict when you tell what you think will happen.

How might scientists predict how many apples will grow? They may think about how many apples grew the year before.

Picture Clues How do you know this apple tree is healthy?

_____

_____

_____

_____

Scientists learn about how plants grow. They learn how to grow more and better apples.

Classify

Scientists classify, or put things in groups. Scientists might classify kinds of apples by taste, shape, and color.

There are many different kinds of apples. How do you know what kinds of apples are the smallest? You might group apples by size.

Compare and Contrast

Scientists compare and contrast what they observe too. They tell what is alike. They tell what is different.

How do you know if red apples are as sweet as green apples?

_____

_____

_____

At-Home Lab

A Good Observer
Observe an apple. Look at it carefully. Feel it. Write what you observe.

13

Lesson 3

How do scientists use tools and stay safe?

Tell one observation the beekeeper might make.

Inquiry **Explore It!**

Which tool works better?

☐ **1.** Use both tools. **Measure** the thickness of a book. Measure the height of a desk. Measure the length of your chalkboard.

☐ **2.** **Record** your data in the chart.

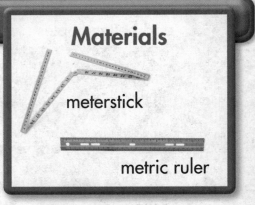

Materials

meterstick

metric ruler

	Measurement (cm)	Which tool worked better?
Thickness of book		
Height of desk		
Length of chalkboard		

Explain Your Results

3. Communicate Did the same tool always work better? Explain.

_____

_____

_____

_____

Word to Know

tool

Tools

Scientists use many different kinds of tools. A **tool** is something that is used to do work.

Some tools make objects look bigger. A hand lens helps a scientist observe a bee up close. Scientists use tools to stay safe too. A bee scientist wears a face cover and a body cover. The scientist wears gloves too.

Look at the picture of the bee. **Tell** what the bee's wings look like under the hand lens.

Use a hand lens to look at this picture. **Draw** what you see.

You can use a hand lens to study insects.

15

More Tools

You use many different kinds of tools to learn. Some tools are used to measure. Some tools help you stay safe. Read about the tools on these pages.

(Circle) two tools that are used to measure length.

A **thermometer** measures temperature. Most thermometers have a Celsius and a Fahrenheit scale. Most scientists use the Celsius scale.

You can use a **meterstick** to measure how long something is. Scientists use a meterstick to measure in centimeters.

You can use a **ruler** to measure how long something is too. Most scientists use a ruler to measure in centimeters or millimeters. You can use a ruler to measure in inches too.

You can use **safety goggles** to protect your eyes.

You can use a **magnet** to see if an object is made of certain metals.

S

N

LAP   START/STOP   ON/RESET

A **stopwatch** or **timer** measures how long something takes.

95 96 97 98 99

A **pan balance** is used to measure how much mass an object has. Objects that have a lot of mass feel heavy. Objects that do not have a lot of mass feel light.

8 OZ — 240CC
8 OZ — 240CC
7 OZ — 210CC
6 OZ — 180CC
5 OZ — 150CC
4 OZ — 120CC
3 OZ — 90CC
2 OZ — 60CC
1 OZ — 30CC

You can use a **measuring cup** to measure volume. Volume is how much space something takes up.

Tell one way people might use a measuring cup at home.

17

Observe with Tools

Groups of scientists record the steps they take to answer questions. Another group of scientists may follow these steps. They should get the same answers if they follow the same steps and use the same tools.

Scientists compare what they observe with other scientists. Sometimes scientists get different answers. This might happen if a measuring tool is not used correctly. This might happen if the object being measured changes too. Scientists measure more than once to be sure their answers are correct.

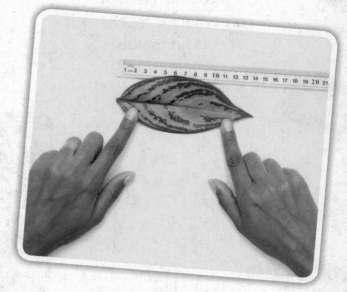

Look at the picture. How long is the leaf? (Circle) the number on the ruler.

At-Home Lab

Measure Temperature
Use a thermometer to measure the outside temperature. Record the temperature in Fahrenheit and Celsius.

Use a measuring cup to measure two liquids.

OZ

Compare your measurements with a partner's measurements.

Safety Tips

Use these tips to stay safe when you observe.

- Listen to your teacher's instructions.
- Never taste or smell materials.
- Wear safety goggles when needed.
- Tie your hair back when needed.
- Handle tools carefully.
- Keep your workplace neat and clean.
- Clean up spills immediately.
- Wash your hands well after every activity.

Circle the tips that are hardest for you to remember.

Draw an X on two ways these people are staying safe.

How do scientists find answers?

Envision It!

This scientist takes samples of the grass every year. **Tell** how the grass might change.

Inquiry Explore It!

What conclusion can you draw?

☐ **1.** Have a partner pick up the chips one at a time and put them in the cup.

☐ **2.** Count the number of seconds that pass. **Record** how long it took to move all the chips.

Materials

chips   plastic cup

Explain Your Results

3. Draw a Conclusion If you did this again, would you have the same result? Explain.

_____
_____
_____
_____

4. How could you improve your test?

_____
_____
_____

Words to Know

conclusion
hypothesis

Repeat Investigations

Scientists learn about the world around them. First they ask questions. Then they investigate. You investigate when you look for answers.

Scientists repeat investigations before they draw conclusions. A **conclusion** is what you decide after you think about all you know. You should be able to draw similar conclusions when you repeat an investigation.

Scientists make conclusions from what they learn when they investigate.

For example, one scientist measures the height of the tallest tree in a forest. Others repeat the measurement. They get similar answers. They draw a conclusion.

Explain what would happen if other people repeat the same investigation as the scientist in the picture.

21

Scientific Methods

Scientific methods are ways of finding answers. Some scientists use scientific methods when they do experiments. Scientific methods may have these steps. Sometimes scientists do the steps in a different order. Scientists do not always do all of the steps.

Ask a question.

Ask a question that you want answered.

Do seeds need water to grow?

Make your hypothesis.

A **hypothesis** is a possible answer to your question.

If seeds are watered, then they will grow because seeds need water.

Plan a fair test.

Change only one thing. Keep everything else the same. Record your steps. Someone else should get the same answer if they follow your steps.

Use the same kinds of pots and soil. Water only one pot.

Write the words water and no water to label the pots.

Do your test.

Test your hypothesis. Repeat your test. See if your results are the same.

Collect and record your data.

Keep records of what you observe. Use words, numbers, or drawings to help.

Go Green

Repeat a Test
Do plants need sunlight? Think of a hypothesis. Plan a test. Test your hypothesis. Record your steps. Repeat your test.

Tell your conclusion.

Think about the results of your test. Decide if your hypothesis is supported or not supported. Tell what you decide.

Seeds need water to grow.

Circle the question. **Underline** the hypothesis.

Explain what you think would happen if someone else followed the same steps in this investigation.

_____

_____

_____

_____

Lesson 5

How do scientists collect and share data?

Envision It!

Write what you observe about the rocks.

Inquiry **Explore It!**

What are different ways you can collect and share data?

How many boys and girls are in your class?

☑ **1.** Use the Tally Chart.

Make 1 mark for each boy.

Make 1 mark for each girl.

Tally Chart	
Boys	
Girls	

☑ **2.** Use the Picture Chart.

Color 1 picture for each boy.

Color 1 picture for each girl.

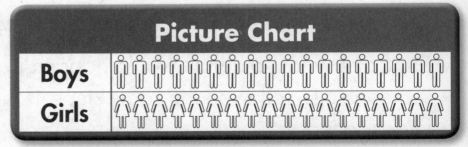

Picture Chart	
Boys	
Girls	

Explain Your Results

3. Communicate Share your charts with your family. Which did they like better? Explain.

_____

Word to Know

data

Collect Data

Scientists collect data to learn new things. **Data** is what you observe. You use your senses to collect data.

Scientists make conclusions from the data and from what they already know. Scientists infer when they make conclusions. You infer when you use what you know to explain something.

<u>**Underline**</u> what you use to observe data.

◉ **Picture Clues Look** at the picture. What can you infer about the rocks?

Record Data

Scientists record what they observe and measure. They look at the data carefully.

Scientists can learn new things when they record data. Sometimes they find patterns. Sometimes they learn what is the same. Sometimes they learn what is different.

Look at the three rocks.
Measure how wide each rock is with a ruler.
Write the data in centimeters.

granite

basalt

pumice

Show Data

Scientists use charts and graphs to show data. A chart helps you organize data. A bar graph helps you compare data.

Use your data. **Fill in** this empty chart.

Comparing Rocks	
	Width (centimeters)
Granite	
Basalt	
Pumice	

Use this empty bar graph. **Fill in** the bar for each rock.

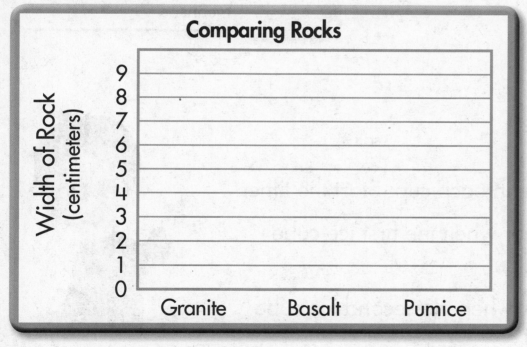

Make a conclusion from your data.
Which rock is the widest?

What skills do scientists use?

Materials

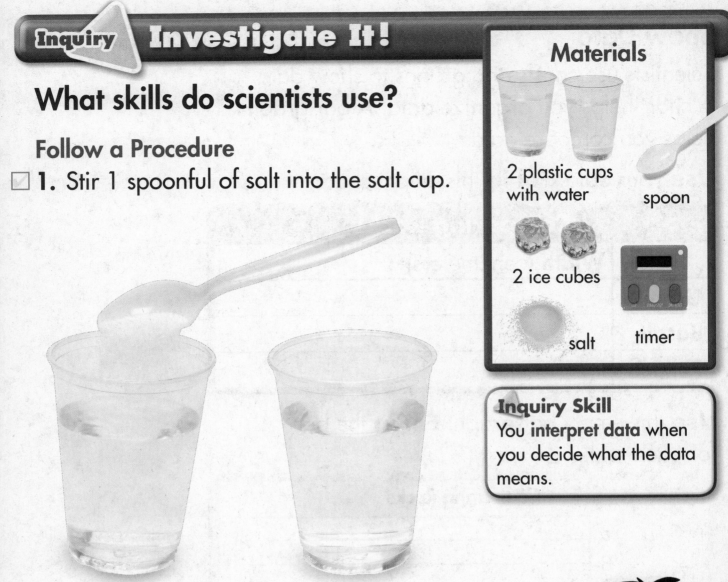

2 plastic cups with water

spoon

2 ice cubes

salt

timer

Follow a Procedure

☑ **1.** Stir 1 spoonful of salt into the salt cup.

plain   salt

Inquiry Skill
You **interpret data** when you decide what the data means.

☑ **2.** Put 1 ice cube in each cup. Start the timer.

☑ **3.** Check the timer when the first ice cube melts. **Record.**

☑ **4.** Stop the timer when the second ice cube melts. Record.

Ice Cube Data	
	Time to Melt (minutes)
Plain water	
Salt water	

Analyze and Conclude

5. Interpret Data Did the ice cubes melt at the same rate? Explain.

_____

_____

_____

_____

6. UNLOCK THE BIG ? Name three science skills you used.

_____

_____

_____

_____

Biography
Read Together

Shonte Wright

Shonte Wright knew she wanted to be a scientist and work at NASA when she was ten years old. She took many math and science classes to help her get ready for the job.

In 2003 NASA sent two robots to Mars. The robots were called rovers. Shonte Wright helped make sure the rovers would still work after the long trip through space.

Tell one question Shonte Wright might have asked about the rovers.

Rovers took pictures of Mars and sent them back to Earth. NASA used the pictures to study the planet.

Vocabulary Smart Cards

inquiry
observe
tool
conclusion
hypothesis
data

Play a Game!

Cut out the cards.

Work with a partner.

One person puts the cards picture side up.

The other person puts the cards picture side down.

Work together to match each word with its meaning.

conclusion

conclusión

inquiry

indagación

hypothesis

hipótesis

observe

observar

data

datos

tool

instrumento

asking questions and looking for answers

hacer preguntas y buscar respuestas

what you decide after you think about all you know

lo que decides después de pensar en lo que sabes

to use your senses to find out about something

usar tus sentidos para descubrir algo

a possible answer to a question

respuesta posible a una pregunta

something that is used to do work

algo que se usa para hacer trabajo

what you observe

lo que observas

Lesson 1

What questions do scientists ask?

- Scientists use inquiry to learn about things.
- Scientists discover ways to solve problems.

Lesson 2

What kinds of skills do scientists use?

- Scientists observe and predict.
- Scientists classify and compare.

Lesson 3

How do scientists use tools and stay safe?

- Scientists use many different tools to learn.
- Hand lenses, rulers, and gloves are tools.

Lesson 4

How do scientists find answers?

- Scientists investigate and draw conclusions.
- A hypothesis is a possible answer to a question.

Lesson 5

How do scientists collect and share data?

- Scientists use their senses to collect data.
- Scientists show data in charts and bar graphs.

Chapter Review

Lesson 1

◎ **1. Picture Clues** The girl in the picture is using inquiry to learn about plants. What is she learning about the plant?

_____

_____

2. Apply Some scientists ask questions about space. **Write** a question you have about space.

_____

_____

_____

_____

Lesson 2

3. Vocabulary **Complete** the sentence.

You _____ when you use your senses to find out about something.

4. Describe **Look** at the picture. **Write** something you observe about this rock.

_____

_____

_____

Lesson 3

5. Classify What is a tool that can help you stay safe?
Fill in the bubble.

Ⓐ meterstick   Ⓒ goggles

Ⓑ stopwatch   Ⓓ magnet

Lesson 4

6. Evaluate Why might a scientist repeat investigations?

_____

- -

_____

Lesson 5

7. Analyze Look at the picture.
What can you infer about this plant?

_____

- -

_____

Got it?

◻ **Stop!** I need help with _____

_____

- -

▶ **Go!** Now I know _____

How do computers help you?

Technology and Tools

Try It!   How can you keep an ice cube from melting?

Lesson 1   What is technology?

Lesson 2   How do people design new things?

Lesson 3   How do we use tools and machines?

Investigate It!   How can a machine ring a bell?

Tell how you use a computer.
Tell about another kind of technology that is important to you.

How do people solve problems?

Go to www.myscienceonline.com and click on:

Untamed Science
Ecogeeks answer your questions.

Got it? 60-Second Video
Take one minute to learn science!

Envision It!
See what you already know about science.

Science Songs
Sing along with animated science songs!

How can you keep an ice cube from melting?

☐ **1.** Put an ice cube in each of 2 cups.

☐ **2. Design** a way to keep an ice cube from melting. Make and test your design.

☐ **3.** Wait 10 minutes. **Observe.** Compare the 2 ice cubes.

_____
- - - - - - - - - - - - - - - - - -
_____
- - - - - - - - - - - - - - - - - -
_____

Explain Your Results

4. Communicate
   Draw and label your **design.**

Materials

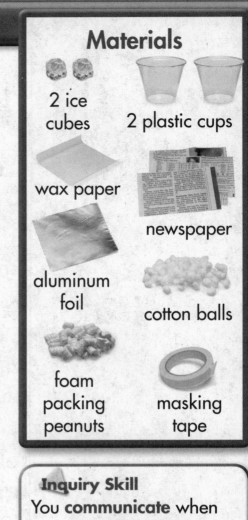

2 ice cubes

2 plastic cups

wax paper

newspaper

aluminum foil

cotton balls

foam packing peanuts

masking tape

Inquiry Skill
You **communicate** when you draw and label diagrams.

Main Idea and Details

The **main idea** is the most important idea in what you are reading. **Details** tell about the main idea.

Telephones

Telephones have changed. Long ago, most telephones were attached to a wall by wires. Today you can carry a telephone with you. Telephones are much smaller and lighter today than they were years ago.

Practice It!

Write two details about how telephones have changed.

Telephones have changed over the years.

Main Idea

Detail

Detail

What is technology?

Envision It!

Tell what problem the train helps solve.

MY PLANET DIARY

INVENTION!

Read Together

Engineers have designed a train that uses magnets instead of engines. These trains are called Maglev trains. They are faster and quieter than trains that use engines. Maglev trains float about one to ten centimeters above a guideway. The magnets on the bottoms of the trains and the magnets on the guideway help move the train along. Maglev trains can travel faster than 300 miles per hour!

Use a ruler. **Draw** a line that is ten centimeters tall to show how high Maglev trains can float.

guideway

Words to Know
....
technology
invent

Technology

People ride in cars. People use computers. We can do these things because of technology. **Technology** is the use of science to solve problems.

Sometimes people use technology to invent things. **Invent** means to make something for the first time.

Technology has made many things easier for people. Cars and trains are technology. They help people travel long distances. However, technology does not solve every problem. Cars and trains can break and stop working.

Tell one way computers help people. **Tell** one problem computers do not solve.

Scientists make cars that use electricity. These cars help reduce pollution.

41

Solve Problems

Engineers are people who design new things. They look for better ways to solve problems. They use science and technology to invent and discover new things.

Some people have trouble seeing. People used technology to solve this problem. People invented glasses. Glasses help people see better. Glasses are technology.

⊙ **Main Idea and Details Underline** a problem that technology solves.

Read about technology below. **Pick** one technology. **Tell** what kind of problem it solves.

Technology Over Time

1879
The light bulb is mass-produced.

1885
A car that uses gasoline is invented.

1903
The Wright brothers fly their plane in Kitty Hawk, North Carolina.

1946
The first microwave oven is built.

Help People

Technology can help people stay healthy too. Doctors use technology to find out why people are sick.

People invented X rays. X rays are tools doctors can use to see inside people. Doctors can help people to get well after they find out what is wrong.

Draw another kind of technology. **Tell** what problem it solves. **Tell** one problem it does not solve.

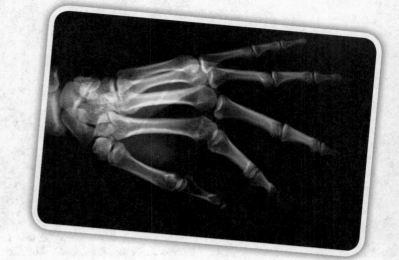

1975
The digital camera is invented.

2008
Text messaging is popular.

Draw something you would like to invent.

Lesson 2

How do people design new things?

Tell what you might like to design.

Inquiry **Explore It!**

How can you keep warm water warm?

☐ **1.** Fill 2 cups with warm water. **Measure** both temperatures. **Record.**

☐ **2.** **Cover** one with foil, plastic, or a paper towel.

☐ **3.** Wait 10 minutes. Measure. Record.

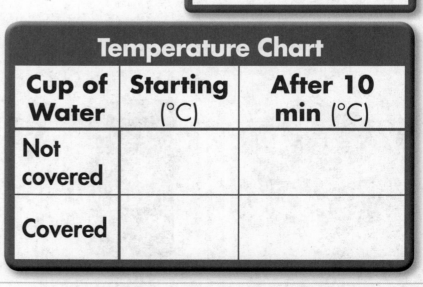

Materials

warm water

plastic wrap

tape

paper towel

foil

2 cups

thermometer

Temperature Chart

Cup of Water	Starting (°C)	After 10 min (°C)
Not covered		
Covered		

Explain Your Results

4. Infer How did you keep the water warm?

_____

_____

44

Words to Know

goal
material

A Problem and a Goal

Engineers think about a problem that needs to be solved. Then they set a goal to find a solution to the problem. A **goal** is something you want to do.

Chester Greenwood lived a long time ago in Maine. Chester had a problem. His ears got very cold in the winter. He set a goal. He wanted to find a way to keep his ears warm.

Maine can get very cold in the winter.

Think about a problem you want to solve. **Write** your goal.

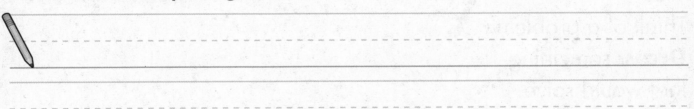

Plan and Draw

Engineers plan and draw before they make new things. Sometimes they plan and draw more than once.

Chester Greenwood planned to use a heavy wool scarf to stay warm. He tied it around his head. It kept his ears warm. However, the wool scarf was very itchy.

Chester wanted to find a better solution to his problem. Chester planned again. He planned to make earflaps to cover his ears.

Look at the drawings to see what Chester's plan might have looked like.

1. Make wire loops.   2. Cover loops.   3. Sew covers around wire loops.

Think of a problem. **Draw** something that would solve the problem. **Tell** how it solves your problem.

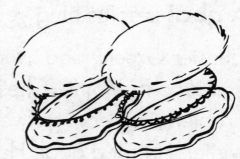

Choose Materials

Engineers choose materials to make new things. A **material** is what something is made of. Materials can be very different. Some materials are soft. Other materials are hard. Some materials are light. Other materials are heavy.

(Circle) materials you would want to use to keep your ears warm. **Tell** why.

At-Home Lab

Different Designs
Find out about two kinds of shoes. What are the shoes used for? Tell how the designs are different.

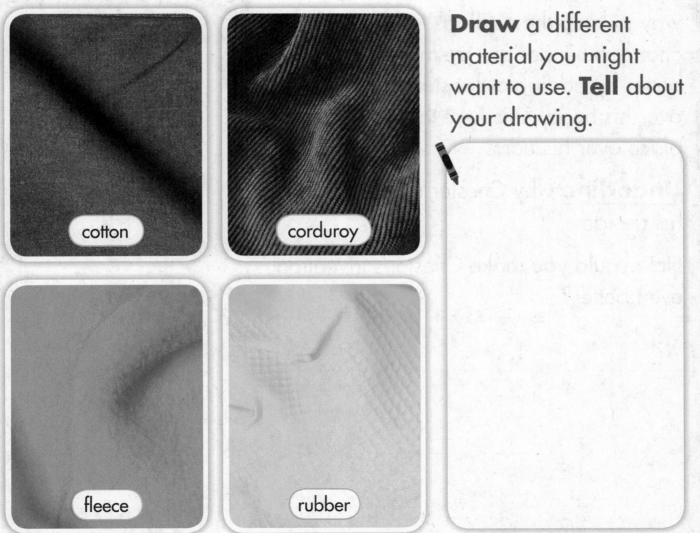

cotton

corduroy

fleece

rubber

Draw a different material you might want to use. **Tell** about your drawing.

Make and Test

Engineers make and test the solution to their problem. They want to find out how well their design works. Sometimes they change their design. They do this to make their design better.

Chester made oval loops out of wire. Then he covered the loops with soft materials. Chester's earflaps kept his ears warm.

However, Chester wanted to find a better way to keep the earflaps in place. He changed his design. He made his design better by adding a flat steel spring to fit over his head. This kept the earflaps in place over his ears.

Underline why Chester changed his design.

How could you make Chester's invention even better?

_____
_____
_____
_____
_____

Record and Share

Engineers record what they have done. They write about their designs. They draw and label their designs too. Recording helps them remember what they have done. Sometimes engineers share what they have done with others.

Write headband or earflap to label the parts of these earmuffs.

This girl is wearing earmuffs. There are many different kinds of earmuffs today.

49

Lesson 3

How do we use tools and machines?

Envision It!

Tell what kinds of tools you think were used to build this tree house.

Inquiry Explore It!

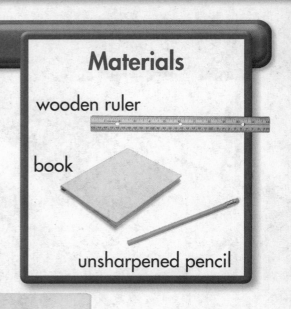

Materials

wooden ruler

book

unsharpened pencil

How does a lever work?

A lever is a type of simple machine.

☐ **1.** Make a lever. Set up the ruler, pencil, and book as shown.

☐ **2.** Push down on the end of the lever. **Observe.**

☐ **3.** Repeat with the pencil at 15 cm and at 10 cm.

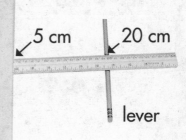

5 cm   20 cm

lever

Explain Your Results

4. Communicate When was it easiest to lift the book?

_____

_____

_____

UNLOCK
THE BIG
?
I will know about tools and simple machines. I will know how some body parts can be used as tools.

Words to Know
....
simple machine

Tools and Machines

Suppose you want to move an object. You might use a tool to help you. A machine is a tool that can make work easier. Sometimes tools and machines can do things that your body cannot do on its own.

A **simple machine** is a tool with few or no moving parts. A screw is a simple machine. A screw is used to hold things together.

A wagon is a machine. You can use a wagon to move heavy things. You can use a wagon to move many things at one time.

Draw one object that is held together by screws.

51

Simple Machines

There are many different kinds of tools and machines. Levers and wedges are simple machines. Pulleys and inclined planes are simple machines too.

pulley

Pulleys move an object up, down, or sideways. An inclined plane is flat. It is higher at one end than at the other. An inclined plane makes it easier to move things.

Look at the picture below. **Circle** the part that is the inclined plane.

Tell how the pulley moves the flag.

Suppose you need to move a heavy box. What could you use to help you move it? **Design** a tool to help you.

Body Parts as Tools

Think about different parts of your body.
You can use some parts of your body as
tools. You can use your body to do work.

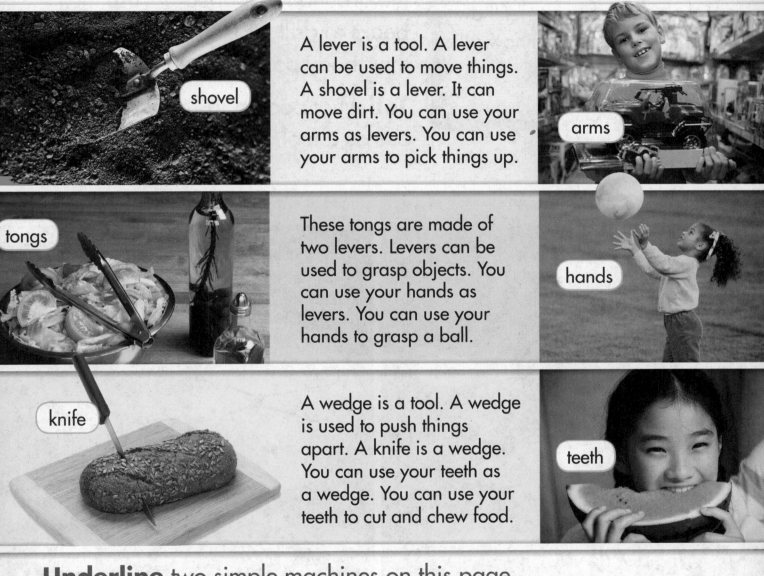

A lever is a tool. A lever can be used to move things. A shovel is a lever. It can move dirt. You can use your arms as levers. You can use your arms to pick things up.

shovel

arms

These tongs are made of two levers. Levers can be used to grasp objects. You can use your hands as levers. You can use your hands to grasp a ball.

tongs

hands

A wedge is a tool. A wedge is used to push things apart. A knife is a wedge. You can use your teeth as a wedge. You can use your teeth to cut and chew food.

knife

teeth

Underline two simple machines on this page.

What other body part can you use as a tool? **Explain.**

Lightning Lab

Tools in Nature
Make a model of an animal body part. Tell how it is like a tool. Tell how it is different from a tool.

Animal Body Parts as Tools

Think about different animals. Animals use body parts as tools. Gophers use their claws to dig into the ground. Woodpeckers use their beaks to drill into trees. Animals use their body parts to do work.

Tell what body parts a dog might use as a tool.

The beaver has long front teeth. It uses its teeth as a wedge to cut into wood.

teeth

wedge

The blue jay uses its beak to hold on to food. Its beak is like two levers.

levers

beak

Draw another animal that can use body parts as tools. **Tell** about the animal you drew.

The sea turtle uses its flippers as shovels, or levers. It kicks sand out of the way to build a nest.

lever

flippers

Badger claws are like wedges. The claws help the badger dig into the ground.

wedge

claws

How can a machine ring a bell?

Follow a Procedure

☑ **1. Design** a way to ring a bell from one meter away. Use two simple machines.

☑ **2.** Draw your plan.

Materials

bell

marble

common objects

meterstick

Inquiry Skill
You **infer** when you get ideas from what you learn.

☐ **3. Record** what materials you will use.

☐ **4.** Test your design.
My machine **(did / did not)** ring the bell.

☐ **5.** Evaluate your design. How could you **redesign** your machine to ring the bell better?

Analyze and Conclude

6. Communicate   What simple machines did you use?

----

7. **Infer**   Think how you used a simple machine to solve a problem. How do simple machines help people solve problems?

STEM
Read Together

Microchips

Microchips are everywhere! They are in e-book readers and microwaves. They are in computers too. Microchips are usually less than 1 centimeter on each side. A pea is less than 1 centimeter on each side too.

Engineers use microchips to develop new technology. Microchips let engineers make smaller computers. Microchips help computers give and take directions. For example, many runners use a small computer that has a microchip. The microchip shows how long it took the runner to run the race.

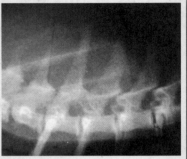

Microchips can help track lost dogs and cats. These chips are about the size of a grain of rice.

What new technology do you think engineers will develop soon?

Vocabulary Smart Cards

technology
invent
goal
material
simple
machine

Play a Game!

Cut out the cards.

Work with a group.

Tape a card to the back of each group member.

Give each person clues about his or her word.

Have everyone guess his or her word.

material

material

technology

tecnología

simple machine

máquina simple

invent

inventar

goal

objetivo

the use of science to solve problems

el uso de la ciencia para resolver problemas

what something is made of

de lo que está hecho algo

to make something for the first time

hacer algo por primera vez

tool with few or no moving parts

instrumento sin, o con pocas, partes que se mueven

something you want to do

algo que quieres hacer

Study Guide

 How do people solve problems?

Lesson 1

What is technology?

- Technology is the use of science to solve problems.
- Invent means to make something for the first time.

Lesson 2

How do people design new things?

- People set a goal, plan, draw, choose materials, make, test, record, and share.

Lesson 3

How do we use tools and machines?

- Simple machines can make work easier.
- You can use some parts of your body as tools.

REVIEW
THE BIG
?

How do people solve problems?

Lesson 1

1. **Describe** **Think** about one kind of technology you use. **Write** how it helps you.

_____

_____

_____

⊙ 2. **Main Idea and Details** **Read** the paragraph below. <u>**Underline**</u> two details.

Technology has changed the way people have fun. People listen to music on MP3 players. People use computers to play games.

Lesson 2

3. **Vocabulary** **Complete** the sentence. **Fill in** the bubble. Chester Greenwood wanted to find a way to keep his ears warm. He set a _____.

Ⓐ problem   Ⓒ goal
Ⓑ record   Ⓓ test

4. **Evaluate** **Circle** the earmuffs that you would want to wear. **Tell** why.

Lesson 3

5. **Classify Draw** a line from the picture to the term that goes with it.

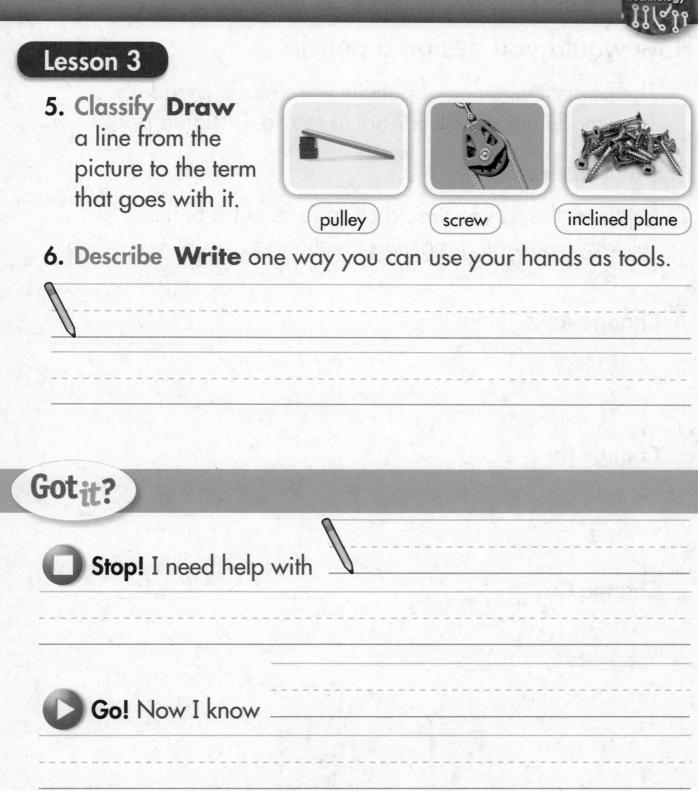

pulley   screw   inclined plane

6. **Describe Write** one way you can use your hands as tools.

_____

_____

_____

Got it?

☐ **Stop!** I need help with _____

_____

_____

▶ **Go!** Now I know _____

_____

_____

Design It!

How would you design a pencil?

The earliest versions of pencils were made by adults.
They made the pencils for adults to use. **Design** a pencil.

Find a problem.

☑ **1.** List three things you would change about a pencil.
Tell why you would make each change.

Change A:

Change B:

Change C:

Plan and draw.

☑ **2.** Pick one thing to change. Make a step-by-step plan.
You will use the materials from the next page.
Tell how you would test your **design.**

_____

- -

_____

_____

_____

- -

_____

_____

- -

_____

☑ **3.** Draw your design. Label each material.

Choose materials.

☐ **4.** Circle the materials you will use.

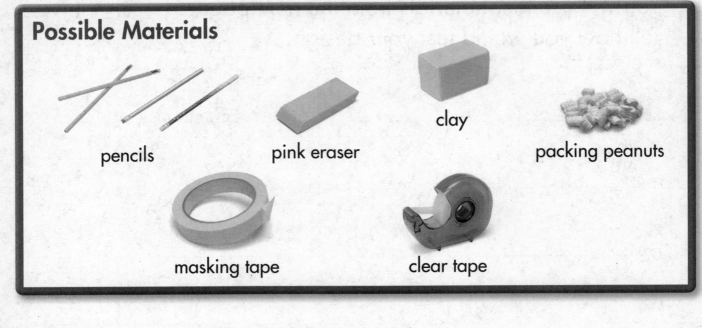

Possible Materials

pencils

pink eraser

clay

packing peanuts

masking tape

clear tape

☐ **5.** Tell how you will use each material.

_____

_____

_____

_____

_____

Make and test.

☐ **6.** Make the new pencil you **designed.** Follow your plan.

☐ **7.** Test your pencil design by filling in the chart below.
Use a regular pencil. Then use the pencil you designed.

Pencil Chart		
	Regular Pencil	**Pencil You Designed**
Print Pencil. **Pencil**		
Handwrite Pencil. *Pencil*		
Print $3 + 5 = 8$. $3 + 5 = 8$		
Draw the hammer. 		

Record and share.

☐ **8.** Use your new pencil for one day.
   Record when you used your pencil.
   Record your **observations** about how well it worked.

☐ **9.** What about your pencil **design** worked well?

_____

_____

_____

_____

☐ **10.** What about your pencil design did not work well?

_____

_____

_____

_____

☐ **11.** How could you **redesign** your pencil?

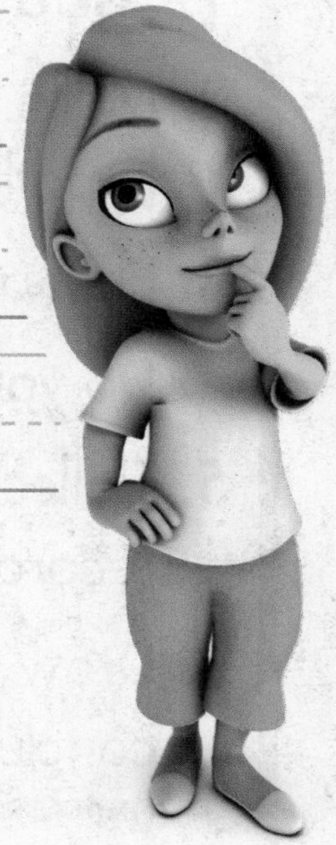

_____

_____

_____

_____

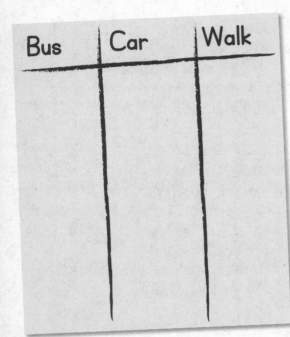

Bus	Car	Walk

Travel to School

- Do more classmates come to school on a bus, in a car, or by walking?

- Make a hypothesis.

- Use a chart and collect data.

Design a Solution

- Think of a problem you want to solve.

- Plan and draw your solution in a notebook.

- Label your drawing.

- List the materials you would use.

- Share your design with a partner.

Write a Song

- Write a song about technology.

- Give your song a name and sing it to the class.

Using Scientific Methods

1. Ask a question.
2. Make a hypothesis.
3. Plan a fair test.
4. Do your test.
5. Collect and record data.
6. Draw a conclusion.

Life
Science

How is a giraffe like a zebra?

Plants and Animals

Try It! What do plants need to be healthy?

Investigate It! How does water affect plant growth?

Draw an X on two things that the giraffe needs. **Tell** how your needs and a giraffe's needs are alike.

THE BIG ? How do plants, animals, and people live in their habitat?

Go to www.myscienceonline.com and click on: ⊗

UntamedScience
Go on a science adventure with the Ecogeeks!

Got it? 60-Second Video
Everything you learned in 60 seconds!

What do plants need to be healthy?

☐ **1.** Put 10 seeds in Cup A.
Put 80 seeds in Cup B.

☐ **2.** Cover the seeds with soil.
Add 4 spoonfuls of water.

Put the cups in sunlight.

Add 1 spoonful of water every day.

☐ **3. Observe** How do the plants look after 3 weeks?

After 3 weeks
the Plants will
may be grow and
get leaves.

Explain Your Results

4. Which plants look healthier?

Plant A is healthier
becaus plant B too much seeds.

5. Draw a Conclusion What is one thing plants need to be healthy?

Plant need water, Air, sunligh
soil

Materials

90 radish seeds

spoon

plastic cup with water

A B 2 paper cups with soil

Inquiry Skill When you collect data, you show what you **observe.**

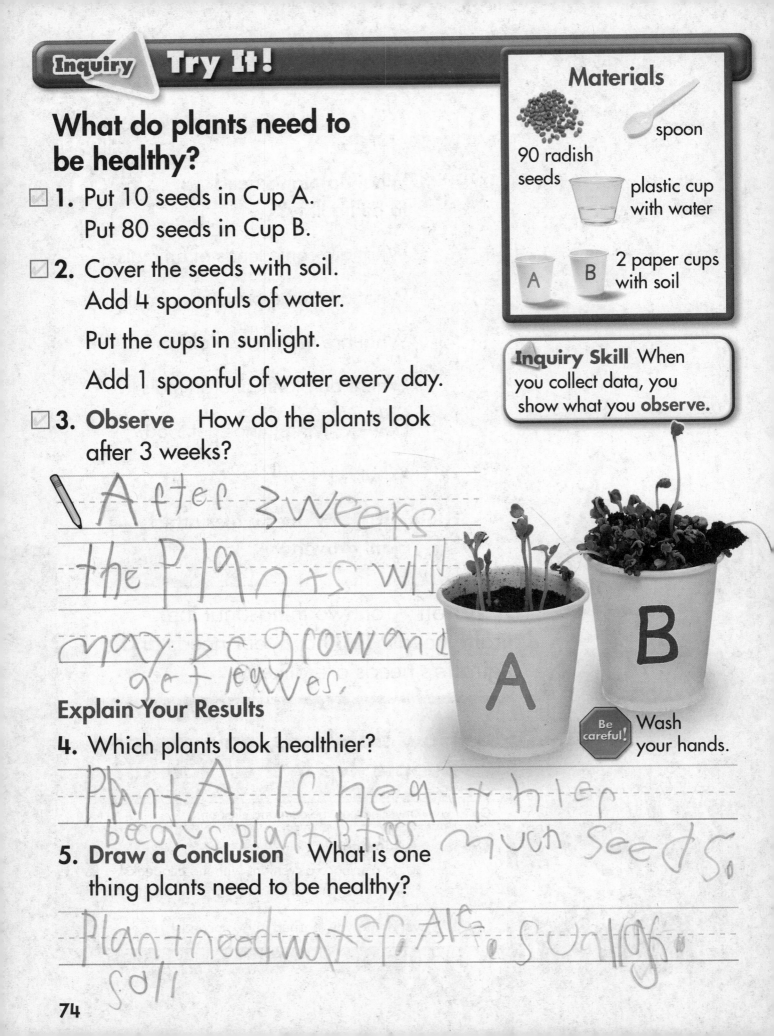

Be careful! Wash your hands.

74

⊙ Compare and Contrast

Compare means to tell how things are alike. **Contrast** means to tell how things are different.

Whales and Fish

Whales and fish live in the ocean. Fish get oxygen from the water. Whales must come to the surface to breathe. Whales get oxygen from the air, like you.

This Southern Right Whale is coming up for air.
▽

Practice It!

Compare and **contrast** whales and fish.

Compare	Contrast
They both live In water. they	the whales blow water out there hole on top of there eteks. anyfish don't

What are some kinds of animals?

Envision It!

Tell how you could sort these animals into groups.

my planet diary

Did You Know?

Read Together

Fish are not the only animals in the ocean. Whales live there too. Whales are not fish. Whales breathe air and feed their babies milk, just like dogs do.

Whales do not look like dogs, though. Whales have side fins called flippers. They have flat tail fins called flukes. Most whales have a fin on their back too. Whales are fast swimmers because they have fins like fish.

Tell how whales and dogs are alike and different.

76

Word to Know

amphibian

Animal Groups

You can group animals by how they look or act. You can group animals by where they live. You can group animals by their body parts. One group of animals has backbones. Another group does not.

You can group snakes and worms together by how they look. Both have long, thin bodies and no legs. But snakes and worms are not the same inside. Snakes have backbones. Worms do not.

garter snake

earthworm

⊙ Compare and Contrast **Write** how snakes and worms are alike and different.

Compare	Contrast
They both sites.	Snakes have backbones and worms don't.

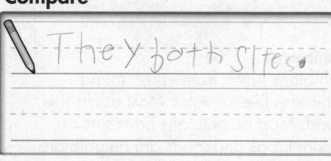

77

Animals with Backbones

Some animals have backbones. Bones help give the animals shape. Bones help the animals move. Bones help protect some body parts. Backbones help some animals grow very big.

Mammals have backbones. Birds and fish have backbones. Reptiles and amphibians have backbones too. An **amphibian** is an animal that lives part of its life in water and part of its life on land.

Write how mammals, birds, fish, reptiles, and amphibians can be grouped together.

how they look how they act and live.

Fish
Fish live in water. Most fish are covered with scales. Fish have fins. Most fish hatch from eggs.

Amphibians
Amphibians hatch from eggs. Young amphibians live in water. Most adults live on land. Most amphibians have smooth, wet skin. Frogs and toads are amphibians.

Birds
Birds have feathers and wings. Birds hatch from eggs. Goldfinches, ducks, and hawks are birds.

Mammals
Mammals usually have hair on their bodies. Young mammals get milk from their mother. Panda bears, dogs, and cats are mammals.

Reptiles
Most reptiles have dry skin and scales. Some reptiles hatch from eggs. Snakes, turtles, and lizards are reptiles.

Draw an **X** on animals that have scales.

Circle an animal that has hair.

Animals Without Backbones

Most animals do not have bones in their body. Some of these animals have shells or other structures that give them shape.

This beetle is an insect.

Insects are animals that do not have bones. Insects have three body parts. The body parts are the head, the thorax, and the abdomen. Insects have six legs. Antennae help some insects feel, smell, hear, and taste.

Spiders are animals without backbones too. Spiders are not insects. Spiders have eight legs. Spiders spin webs. The webs catch insects. Spiders eat insects. Many spiders feel, smell, hear, and taste with the hair on their feet.

⊙ **Compare and Contrast Tell** how insects and spiders are alike and different.

Tell how these spiders are alike and different.

abdomen

thorax

head

antennae

At-Home Lab

Group Animals
Find pictures of different kinds of animals. Sort the animals into groups. Use the groups to make a poster. Explain why the animals in each group belong together.

Look at the picture of the insect.
(Circle) the three main body parts.
Draw an X on a body part that helps an insect feel.

Draw another animal that can be grouped with insects.

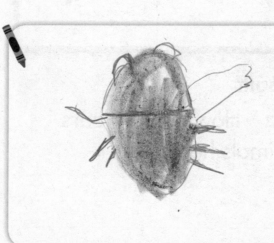

81

Lesson 2

What are some parts of animals?

Circle the part this bird uses to get food.
Tell how you know.

Inquiry **Explore It!**

How do ears compare?

☐ **1.** Click 30 cm from your ear.
Observe. Record what you hear.

☐ **2.** **Make a model** of an elk's big ear.

☐ **3.** **Predict** what will happen if you listen
with your model ear. Repeat.

Observation Human Ear	Prediction Big Ear	Observation Big Ear

Materials

Elk Ear Pattern

elk ear pattern

tape

clicker

metric ruler

Explain Your Results

4. Interpret Data How can big ears
help some animals hear?

animals have big ear
because it can it beter

82

UNLOCK THE BIG ? I will know what animals need. I will know how animals use body parts to meet their needs.

Word to Know

camouflage

Animal Needs

Think of the different kinds of animals in the world. They all have the same needs. A chipmunk has the same needs as a huge whale. It has the same needs as a tiny insect.

Animals need air, water, and food. Animals need shelter. Shelter is a safe place to live and grow. Animals need enough space to live too.

Look at the picture.
Write what need the chipmunk meets.

food water.

83

Animal Body Parts

Animals use their body parts to get what they need. Birds use their beaks to find food. A pelican has a big beak. It scoops up fish with its beak. A woodpecker has a strong, sharp beak. It digs ants and other insects from trees with its beak.

Write why the pelican needs a big beak.

So it can put more theng in there moth.

Look at the shape of the pelican's beak. The beak can hold big fish.

A woodpecker pounds holes in trees with its beak. The holes help the bird find insects.

Lightning Lab

Animal Needs
Find a picture of an animal. Glue it to a sheet of paper. Write what the animal eats. Write how it uses its body parts to get food.

A robin's beak is long and thin. The robin puts its beak into the soil to catch worms.

earthworm

A robin walks or runs on the ground. The robin looks for earthworms to eat.

An earthworm is long and thin. It does not have bones or legs. An earthworm uses its strong muscles to move through the soil.

Write how an earthworm uses its body parts to move.

The earthworm

Tell how a robin uses its body parts to catch earthworms.

Staying Safe

Animals protect themselves in different ways. Some animals have camouflage. **Camouflage** is a color or shape that makes an animal hard to see. Camouflage helps an animal hide from other animals.

Some animals have hard body parts. Some animals have hard shells. They hide in their shells. Some animals have sharp teeth and claws. They use them to bite and scratch. Some animals have sharp spikes or horns. These body parts can protect an animal from getting eaten.

Other animals use poison to stay safe. Some brightly colored frogs have poison in their skin. Animals that want to eat them stay away.

Underline three ways animals protect themselves.

Write how the porcupine fish protects itself.

Pufferfish

Puff because they protect thereselves.

The tiny porcupine fish can make itself big. Its sharp spines stick out when it is big.

86

Protection

This crab spider is hard to see. Its color protects it.

Spikes and horns protect this horned lizard.

This lionfish has poison spines.

The fur of this arctic fox changes colors with the seasons.

Pill bugs roll into a ball. They hide in their hard shells.

Coral snakes bite with poison fangs.

Write labels for each column of the chart.

Tell one thing about an arctic fox. **Tell** one thing about a horned lizard.

What are the parts of plants?

Circle the plant part that brings water from the soil to the stem.

MY PLANET DIARY Did You Know?

The objects in the picture are lithops. Lithops are amazing plants that look like stones. They are often called "living stones." They look so much like stones that they fool many animals. The animals think they are stones and not food.

Lithops can live in very hot and dry places because of their shape. They can store a lot of water in their thick leaves.

leaves

Write how the lithops' shape helps them live in hot, dry places.

The

Words to Know

nutrient

roots

stem

Plant Needs

Plants need water and air to live and grow. Plants need sunlight, space to grow, and nutrients too. A **nutrient** is a food material that living things need to live and grow. Most plants can grow well if they get the right amount of everything they need.

⊙ Sequence **Look** at the picture. The plant is getting water and sunlight. What will happen next?

🖍 The plant will grow and get flowers.

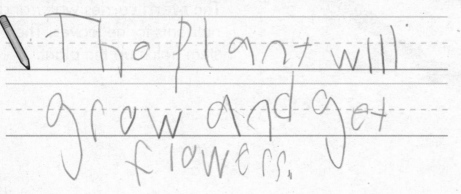

Many plants get nutrients from soil and water.

Plant Parts

Plants have parts. The parts of a plant help
it get what it needs. The parts include roots,
a stem, leaves, flowers, and seeds.

Look at the picture.
Circle a part of the plant that makes food.
Describe each part of the plant.

Green leaves take in sunlight and air.
They use sunlight, air, water, and
nutrients to make food for the plant.

Roots grow down into the soil.
Roots hold the plant in the soil.
Roots take water and nutrients
from the soil to the stem.

The **stem** carries water and
nutrients to the leaves. The
stem holds up the plant.

Some plants have flowers. Flowers make seeds.

Seeds might grow into new plants.

Go Green

Air in Soil

Roots cannot get air when soil is packed too hard. Plant a seed in a cup of loose soil. Plant a seed in a cup of packed soil. Water both and observe. Put your healthy plant in the ground. It will help clean the air.

Draw a plant with flowers. **Label** all of the plant parts.

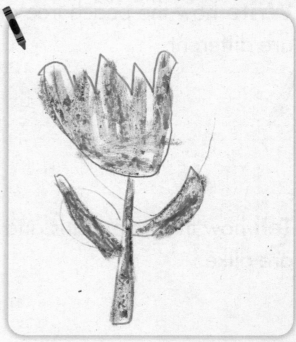

Seed Plants

Most plants are seed plants. Seed plants make seeds and grow from seeds.

Some seed plants have flowers. Many plants with flowers grow fruits. Seeds may grow inside the fruits. The fruits cover and protect the seeds. Fruits and seeds are different shapes and sizes. You can eat the fruit of some seed plants. You can eat a tomato. You cannot eat the fruit of other seed plants. You cannot eat holly berries.

Not all seed plants have flowers. Some seed plants have cones. Seeds grow inside the cones. The cones protect the seeds. Seeds might fall to the ground when the cones open.

Look at the pictures.
Write how the peach tree and the pine tree are different.

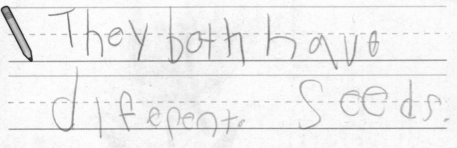

They both have difepent seeds.

Tell how the water lotus and the peach tree are alike.

92

peach
seed

Peach trees grow flowers.
The bottom part of each
flower grows into a fruit
called a peach.

water
lotus seeds

The fruit of the
water lotus forms
the center of the
flower.

pine
seeds

Pine trees have cones that
protect the seeds growing
inside.

93

Where do plants and animals live?

Draw one animal that you think lives in the rain forest.

Inquiry Explore It!

Where can plants live?

☐ **1.** Use a spray bottle.
  Wet 2 paper leaves.

☐ **2.** Cover one with waxed paper.

☐ **3.** Put both in a sunny place.

☐ **4.** Wait 15 minutes. **Observe.**

Materials

paper leaves

spray bottle with water

waxed paper

The waxed paper covers the paper leaf. Some leaves have a waxy cover too.

Explain Your Results

5. Infer How might a waxy coat help a leaf?

to besantand In chen.

6. In what type of habitat might waxy leaves be most helpful to a plant?

It helpes in raly forest

I will know that plants and animals live in habitats that meet their needs.

Word to Know

habitat

Habitats

Living things are found all over Earth. Plants and animals live together in habitats. A **habitat** is the place where a plant or animal lives. Plants and animals live in different kinds of habitats. A habitat can be hot or cold. A habitat can be wet or dry too. Plants and animals can only live in habitats that meet their needs.

This arctic fox lives in the tundra.

Underline where living things can be found.

◉ Picture Clues **Look** at the picture. **Describe** where the arctic fox lives.

It prapry llve lng An

Forest

A forest is a habitat. Forests have many kinds of plants. Many kinds of animals live in the forest too.

Plants and animals get what they need in a forest. They get air and water. Plants get light. Plants get nutrients from the soil. They have space to grow. Some animals find shelter under the trees. Animals eat plants or other animals for food. Living things in a forest depend on one another to get what they need.

Underline where plants get nutrients.
Write where this deer gets the nutrients it needs.

I Leves and grass.

Draw lines from the deer to two things it needs.

This fox uses a log for shelter.

These geese drink water from a pond.

Go Green

Clean Habitats
Living things need air, shelter, and clean water. Tell what happens if the air and water are dirty. Write down three ways to keep habitats clean.

Ocean

An ocean is a habitat. An ocean has salt water. An ocean is large and deep. Many different plants and animals live in the ocean. They get what they need from their habitat. These fish find the food they need in the coral reef.

Write how these fish get what they need.

Plant sand

coral

Desert

Deserts are dry habitats. Some plants and animals can live in the desert. Food and water can be hard to find in the desert.

Cactuses and camels live in some deserts. Cactuses can hold water in their stalks and roots. Fat in its hump helps a camel live in dry places.

Underline how a cactus can live with very little water.

Wetland

A wetland is mostly covered with water. Plants that need a lot of water grow in a wetland.

Plants and animals depend on one another to get what they need in a wetland. Animals eat plants or other animals in a wetland. This alligator eats fish that live in the water.

Tell what kinds of plants grow in a wetland.

Seaweed and flower

sloth

Rain Forest

A rain forest is a wet habitat. It gets a lot of rain. Many trees grow tall to get sunlight. Short plants get little or no sunlight.

Many different animals live in the rain forest. Animals find food and shelter in the rain forest. This sloth gets what it needs from the rain forest.

Look at the picture. **Circle** one thing the sloth needs.

How do living things get food?

Envision It!

Draw what you think will eat the corn.

Inquiry Explore It!

What is the order of a food chain?

☐ **1. Make a model** of a food chain.
   Color the sun on the plate.
   Tape the yarn to the plate.

☐ **2.** Cut apart the cards.
   Tape them in order on the yarn.

Be careful! Be careful with scissors.

Explain Your Results

3. Communicate How did you decide the order of your food chain?

Hawk eats the lizard and lizard eats the bug

Materials

Food Chain Cards

Food Chain Cards

scissors

paper plate

crayons

yarn   tape

Words to Know

food chain   prey
predator

Energy from Food

All plants and animals need food. Most plants make food using sunlight, water, and air. Plants store this food in their leaves, stems, and other parts. Plants use the energy in the food to live and grow.

Animals cannot make food. They must eat plants or other animals. Animals get energy from the food they eat.

◉ **Compare and Contrast** **Write** how the way plants and animals get food is different.

Some animals eat plants other animals eat animals

This rabbit uses energy from the plants it eats to live and grow.

101

Food Chains

A **food chain** shows how energy passes from one living thing to another. The energy in a food chain comes mostly from the sun. Plants use the sun's energy to make food. Some animals get energy by eating the plants. Other animals eat those animals.

Look at the food chain. Energy passes from sunlight to the hawk through this food chain.

Complete the sentence.
Energy in most food chains begins

with the ___Big animals___.

Grasses use water, air, and energy from sunlight to make food.

Voles eat grass for energy.

Predator and Prey

All food chains have predators and prey. A **predator** is an animal that catches and eats another animal. **Prey** is an animal that is caught and eaten. Look at the animals in the food chain. The snake and the hawk are predators.

Draw an X on the snake's prey.

(Circle) the hawk's prey.

Lightning Lab

Draw a Food Chain
Choose a habitat. Draw a food chain that shows how energy passes from one living thing to another in that habitat. Tell about your food chain.

Hawks eat snakes. Snakes are prey for hawks.

Snakes eat voles. Voles are prey for snakes.

103

Lesson 6

What is a fossil?

Envision It!

Draw a line from the fossil to its label.

Inquiry **Explore It!**

What can a fossil show?

Materials

safety goggles

plate with plaster of Paris

paper towels

☐ **1. Make a Model**
Press your hand into the plaster.

☐ **2.** After 60 seconds, remove your hand.

Explain Your Results

3. Draw a Conclusion Look at your **model** fossil. What can you tell about your hand?

Be careful! Wear safety goggles. Wipe your hands when finished. Use a paper towel. Then, wash your hands.

_____

- -

_____

_____

104

leaf   fish   lizard

Words to Know

fossil

extinct

Fossils

A **fossil** is a print or part of a plant or animal that lived long ago. Some fossils are shapes left in rocks. Some are very old bones or teeth. Very old shells and wood can be fossils too.

Dragonflies lived on Earth long ago. Look at the dragonfly fossil. The dragonfly fossil looks like dragonflies that live today.

Tell what fossils can be.

Write the kind of fossil the dragonfly is.

_____

_____

_____

dragonfly fossil

105

A lizard dies.

How Fossils Form

Look at the pictures of the lizard. The pictures show how some fossils form. The lizard dies. Layers of mud and sand cover the lizard. These layers turn to rock after a long time. What is left of the lizard turns to rock too. A print of the lizard is left in the rock.

Write a caption for the second picture. **Complete** the last picture caption.

The layers turn to rock.

This lizard is a _____.

106

What Fossils Show

Fossils show the size and shape of things that lived long ago. Scientists study fossils to see how plants and animals change over time.

Some fossils are of extinct plants and animals. An **extinct** plant or animal no longer lives on Earth. Scientists study fossils for clues about these plants and animals.

Fossils can help scientists learn how Earth has changed. Sometimes scientists find fish fossils in places without water. This tells them that the place once had water.

<u>**Underline**</u> three reasons scientists study fossils.

A fossil can form when tree sap traps an animal. The sap hardens into amber. The animal is still inside.

Tell how amber might help scientists.

This is a dinosaur fossil. Dinosaurs are extinct. Fossils help scientists learn about extinct animals.

How does water affect plant growth?

Follow a Procedure

☐ **1.** Label one cup **water.**
Add water when the soil feels dry.

☐ **2.** Label the other cup **no water.**
Do not add water.

☐ **3. Observe** the plants
daily for 5 days.

Materials

2 bean plants

plastic cup with water

tape

Inquiry Skill
Scientists make careful observations and record them accurately. They use their observations to make **predictions.**

water

no water

☐ **4. Record** your observations below.

Day	Water	No Water
Plant Observations		
Day 1		
Day 2		
Day 3		
Day 4		
Day 5		

Analyze and Conclude

5. UNLOCK THE BIG ? Do plants need water? Explain.

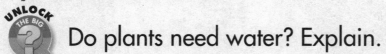

6. **Predict**   What might happen if you watered the **no water** plant? Test your prediction.

Wildlife Rehabilitator

Wildlife rehabilitators know about the needs of animals. They know how the animals live in their habitats.

Wildlife rehabilitators help hurt or sick animals get better and return to the wild. They can even teach young animals how to hunt.

Tell why it is important that wildlife rehabilitators know about the needs of different animals.

This wildlife rehabilitator is taking care of a giant otter pup.

110

Vocabulary Smart Cards

amphibian
camouflage
nutrient
roots
stem
habitat
food chain
predator
prey
fossil
extinct

Play a Game!

Cut out the cards.

Work with a partner. Pick a card. Cover up the word.

Look at the picture and guess the word.

roots

raíces

amphibian

anfibio

stem

tallo

camouflage

camuflaje

habitat

hábitat

nutrient

nutriente

an animal that lives
part of its life in water
and part of its life on
land

animal que pasa
parte de su vida en el
agua y parte en tierra

parts of the plant
that hold the plant
in place and take in
water and nutrients

partes de la planta
que la matienen en su
lugar y que absorben
agua y nutrientes

a color or shape that
makes an animal
hard to see

color o forma que
hace que un animal
se difícil de ver

part of the plant that
carries water and
nutrients to the leaves

parte de la planta
que lleva el agua y
los nutrientes a las
hojas

a material that living
things need to live
and grow

un material que los
seres vivos necesitan
para vivir y crecer

a place where a plant
or animal lives

un lugar donde vive
una planta o un
animal

fossil

fósil

food chain

cadena
alimentaria

extinct

extinto

predator

predador

prey

presa

a model that shows
how energy passes
from one living thing
to another

modelo que muestra
cómo se transmite
la energía de un ser
vivo a otro

a print or part of a
plant or animal that
lived long ago

huella o parte de una
planta o animal que
vivió hace mucho
tiempo

an animal that
catches and eats
another animal

animal que caza y
se alimenta de otro
animal

a plant or animal that
no longer lives on
Earth

planta o animal que
ya no existe en la
Tierra

an animal that is
caught and eaten

animal que es cazado
y comido

REVIEW THE BIG ? How do plants, animals, and people live in their habitat?

Life Science

Lesson 1

What are some kinds of animals?

- Mammals, birds, fish, reptiles, amphibians, and insects are different animal groups.

Lesson 2

What are some parts of animals?

- Body parts help animals get what they need.
- Some animals use camouflage to stay safe.

Lesson 3

What are the parts of plants?

- Plants need nutrients to live and grow.
- Seed plants have roots, stems, and leaves.

Lesson 4

Where do plants and animals live?

- Plants and animals live all around the world.
- A habitat is where a plant or animal lives.

Lesson 5

How do living things get food?

- Most food chains start with the sun.
- Predators catch and eat prey.

Lesson 6

What is a fossil?

- Fossils help scientists learn about the past.
- Extinct plants and animals no longer live on Earth.

Chapter Review

REVIEW THE BIG ? How do plants, animals, and people live in their habitat?

Lesson 1

1. Compare and Contrast Write one way that a bird and a fish are different.

_____

_____

_____

2. Classify A dog, a mouse, and a bear belong to what animal group? **Fill in** the bubble.

Ⓐ amphibian   Ⓒ reptile

Ⓑ mammal   Ⓓ insect

Lesson 2

3. Vocabulary Complete the sentence.
A color or shape that makes an animal hard to see is called

_____

_____ .

Lesson 3

4. Categorize Label the parts of the plant.

_____

_____

_____

Life Science

Lesson 4

5. Identify Draw one animal that lives in a forest habitat and one animal that lives in an ocean habitat.

forest

ocean

Lesson 5

6. Apply Circle the predator in the food chain.
Draw an ✗ on the prey.

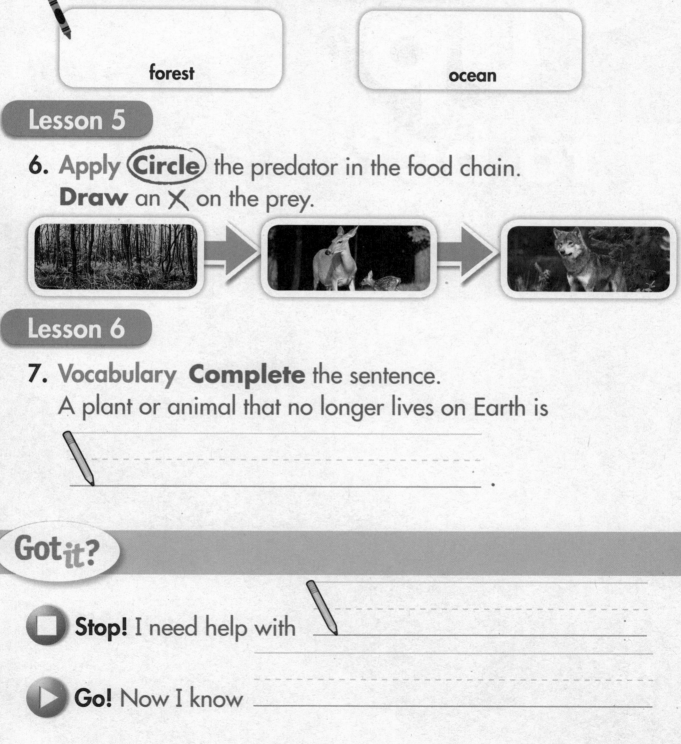

Lesson 6

7. Vocabulary Complete the sentence.
A plant or animal that no longer lives on Earth is

_____

.

Got it?

☐ **Stop!** I need help with _____

_____

▶ **Go!** Now I know _____

What will it grow up to be?

Growing and Changing

Try It! How does a butterfly grow and change?

Investigate It! What is the life cycle of a beetle?

Tell what you think the baby animal will grow up to be.

THE BIG ? How do living things grow and change?

Go to www.myscienceonline.com and click on: ⊗

Untamed Science™
Watch the Ecogeeks in this wild video.

Got it? ⏱ 60-Second Video
Take one minute to learn science!

How does a butterfly grow and change?

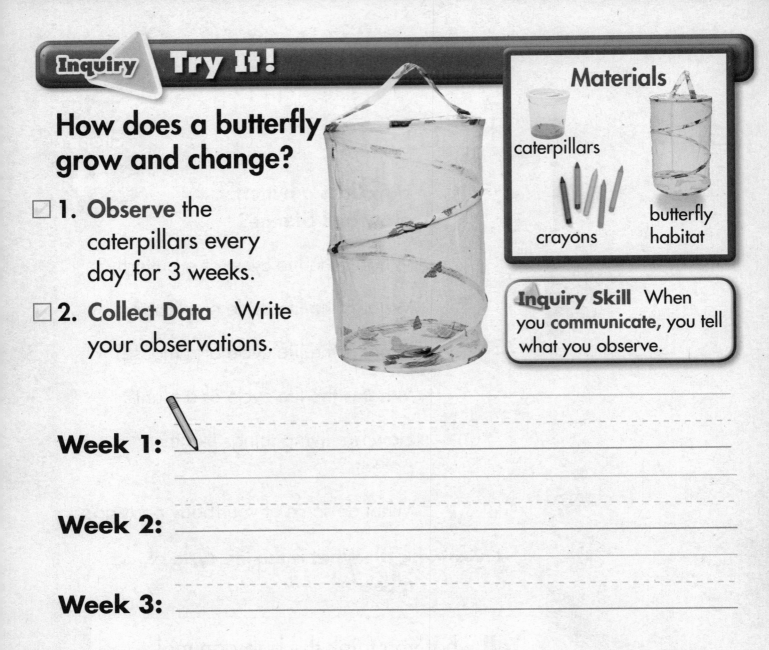

Materials

caterpillars

crayons

butterfly habitat

☐ 1. **Observe** the caterpillars every day for 3 weeks.

☐ 2. **Collect Data** Write your observations.

Inquiry Skill When you **communicate**, you tell what you observe.

Week 1: _____

_____

Week 2: _____

_____

Week 3: _____

Explain Your Results

3. **Communicate** Draw the stages you observed.

Butterfly Growth

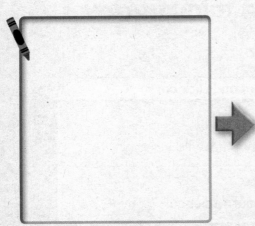

→

→

⊙ Sequence

You put things in **sequence** when you tell what happens first, next, and last.

Life Cycle of a Chicken

First, an adult chicken lays an egg. Next, a chick hatches from the egg. The chick grows and changes. Last, the chick becomes an adult. The adult chicken may lay eggs.

Practice It!

Write which comes first, next, and last.

First

Next

Last

121

What is the life cycle of a butterfly?

The young insect is changing.

MY PLANET DIARY Did You Know?

Zebra longwing butterflies live in warm and humid places like the southeastern United States. These butterflies drink nectar. They feed on pollen too. Eating pollen helps them live longer than most butterflies.

The stripes on the wings of zebra longwing butterflies make it hard to tell if they are coming or going. This makes it hard for other animals to catch them.

Underline what helps zebra longwing butterflies live longer and stay safe.

The zebra longwing caterpillar has spines on its back.

The zebra longwing butterfly makes a creaking sound with its body when disturbed.

Draw what you think will come out.

Words to Know

life cycle
larva
pupa

Butterflies

Butterflies are insects. Insects have six legs. Look at the butterfly. First, it lands on a flower. Next, the butterfly drinks the nectar from the flower. The nectar is food for the butterfly. Last, the butterfly flies away.

This butterfly gets what it needs from the flower.

Butterflies are living things. Living things grow and change. The way a living thing grows and changes is called its **life cycle.** Many young insects look very different when they become adult insects.

◉ **Sequence Write** what happens next and last.

First

A butterfly lands on a flower.

Next

Last

123

Butterfly Life Cycle

Butterflies go through a life cycle. First, the butterfly is a tiny egg. Next, a larva hatches from the egg. A **larva** is a young insect. A butterfly larva is called a caterpillar. Caterpillars eat a lot and grow very quickly.

The caterpillar finds a place to attach itself. A hard covering called a chrysalis grows around the caterpillar. The caterpillar becomes a **pupa.** Wings begin to grow in the pupa stage.

Last, the adult butterfly breaks out of the chrysalis. The butterfly may lay eggs. The life cycle begins again.

Tell about the stages of the butterfly life cycle.

egg

⊙ Sequence **Draw** an X on the stage after the larva stage.

caterpillar

butterfly

pupa

Lightning Lab

Play a Butterfly
You are a butterfly. Take the shape of its egg. You become a caterpillar. Show how you would move. You become a pupa. Take the shape of the pupa. You become a butterfly. Fly around.

125

Lesson 2

What is the life cycle of a frog?

Draw what you think are the stages of the frog's life cycle in order.

Inquiry **Explore It!**

How are life cycles alike and different?

☐ **1.** Put the Butterfly Life Cycle Cards in order. Glue the cards to the plates.

☐ **2.** Put the Frog Life Cycle Cards in order. Glue them to the other side of the plates.

Explain Your Results

3. Compare one stage of each life cycle.

_____

_____

_____

4. Communicate What changed during the frog's life cycle?

_____

_____

Materials

Butterfly and Frog Life Cycle Cards

glue   mobile

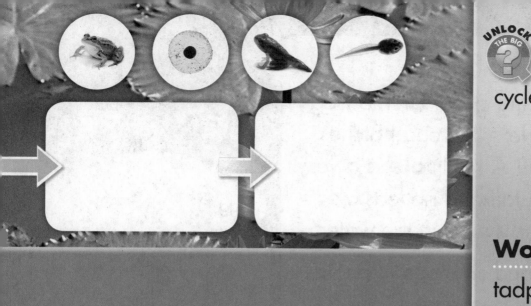

Word to Know

tadpole

Frogs

Frogs are amphibians. An amphibian is an animal that lives part of its life in the water. It lives part of its life on land too.

Very young frogs do not look like their parents. Young frogs go through many changes as they grow.

Underline two places where amphibians live.

Write about a place where a frog might live.

This frog uses its strong legs to escape its enemies.

Frog Life Cycle

Frogs go through a life cycle. First, a frog begins as an egg. Next, the egg hatches. A tadpole swims out! A **tadpole** is a very young frog. It has a tail and no legs. A tadpole breathes and swims in the water.

The tadpole grows and changes. It begins to grow legs. Then, it becomes a young frog. The young frog's legs grow stronger while its tail gets smaller. Last, it grows and changes to become an adult frog.

An adult frog does not have a tail. An adult frog may lay eggs. The life cycle begins again.

Sequence Draw arrows to show the stages of the frog life cycle in order. **Tell** about the stages of the frog life cycle.

egg

adult frog

tadpole

young frog

Lightning Lab

How You Grow Older
Draw pictures of yourself. Put them in order. Begin with a baby picture. Glue the pictures to a large piece of paper. Write down the changes you see.

What is the life cycle of a mouse?

Envision It!

Draw an X on the babies that belong to the mouse.

MY PLANET DIARY

Connections

Read Together

Different kinds of mice live in different places. You might see a deer mouse where you live. You will not find one in China. Deer mice live only in North America.

Long ago, house mice only lived in Asia. Today, they live around the world. How did house mice move to so many places? House mice rode on ships as people explored the world!

Write how the house mice moved around the world.

house mouse

Word to Know

litter

Mice

Mice are mammals. Like other mammals, a mouse has hair on its body. A young mouse gets milk from its mother.

Young mice grow and change. They look more like their parents as they grow. Look at the picture. An adult mouse has big ears and long whiskers. It has a long tail too.

Underline two ways that mice are like other mammals.

Predict how big ears might help a mouse.

Mice cannot see well. They use their whiskers to sense what is around them.

131

Mouse Life Cycle

Mice go through a life cycle. Look at the litter of newborn mice. A **litter** is all the babies born to a mammal at the same time.

A mouse is very tiny when it is born. Its eyes and ears are closed. It does not have hair. Baby mice grow quickly.

When a mouse is two weeks old it looks like its parents. It has hair. Its eyes and ears are open. When a mouse is three weeks old it leaves the nest. Soon the mouse can have babies of its own. The life cycle begins again.

○ **Sequence Tell** what happens to a young mouse before it leaves the nest.

Look at the picture of the newborn mice. **Write** how they look like their parents.

_____

_____

_____

one week

two weeks

newborn

A newborn mouse is different from its parents because it does not have

_____

_____ .

adult

Lightning Lab

Mouse Life Cycle
Work with a partner. Write a sentence that describes a stage of the mouse life cycle. Trade with your partner. Match the sentence to the stage in the mouse life cycle.

Lesson 4

What is the life cycle of a plant?

Envision It!

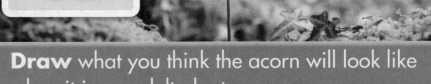

Draw what you think the acorn will look like when it is an adult plant.

Inquiry **Explore It!**

How does a seed grow?

☐ **1.** Put the seeds on the paper towel. Put the towel in the bag.

☐ **2.** Seal the bag. Put it in a warm place.

☐ **3.** **Observe** the seeds every other day. **Record** your observations.

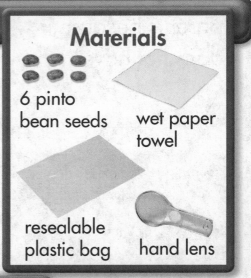

Materials

6 pinto bean seeds   wet paper towel

resealable plastic bag   hand lens

Observations	
Day 1	
Day 3	
Day 5	
Day 7	
Day 9	

Explain Your Results

4. Which parts grew first? **Predict** what will happen next.

_____

- -

_____

Word to Know

seedling

Seeds

Many plants grow from seeds. Fruits cover and protect seeds.

The seeds inside the fruits can be spread in many different ways. Some seeds are spread by air or water. Some seeds are spread by animals. People can spread the seeds into the soil too. New plants might begin to grow.

Underline one reason fruits are important.

Seeds are inside each apple. The fruit of the apple protects the seeds.

Burs are fruits that can travel by hooking onto something.

135

Bean Plant Life Cycle

First, a bean plant is a seed. The seed has a hard covering called a seed coat. The seed coat protects the seed.

Each seed has material that will become a plant. The seed has food for the plant too. A seed that gets enough water and air might begin to grow. Roots grow down into the ground. Next, a young plant grows out of the ground. It is called a **seedling.**

The plant continues to grow. Last, the plant becomes an adult. The adult plant makes seeds. Some seeds will grow into new plants. The life cycle begins again.

Sequence Draw a seed with roots beginning to grow down into the ground.

Go Green

The Good Bean
Plants need nutrients to grow strong. Some plants help add nutrients to soil. Beans do this. Research how planting beans can improve soil. Use your research to make a poster describing why it is good to plant beans.

seed

Flowers grow on the adult bean plant. The flowers make seeds.

Tell about the stages in the life cycle of a bean plant.

adult plant

seedling

How are living things like their parents?

Envision It!

Tell how the cat and kittens are alike. **Tell** how they are different.

Inquiry **Explore It!**

How are babies like their parents?

☐ 1. **Classify** Cut out the cards. Match each parent and baby.

☐ 2. **Observe** each pair. **Record** your observations on the chart.

Explain Your Results

3. **Communicate** Which babies look like their parents?

_____

_____

_____

4. **Interpret Data** How are the babies like their parents?

_____

_____

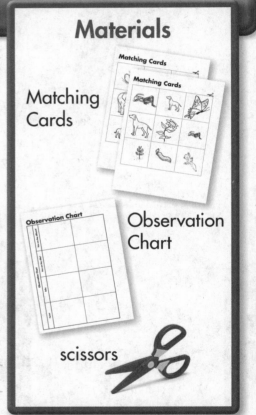

Materials

Matching Cards

Observation Chart

scissors

Word to Know

inherit

Living Things and Their Parents

Living things often look like their parents in some ways. They might inherit their shape from their parents. They might inherit their color. **Inherit** means to get from a parent. Living things may look different from their parents in some ways too.

Look at the family in the picture. **Write** one way the children are like their parents.

_____

_____

_____

Tell one way they are different.

139

Animals and Their Parents

Young animals often look like their parents. A young giraffe inherits its long neck from its parents. It inherits its spots too.

Animals can look different from their parents too. Each giraffe has its own pattern of spots. No two patterns are the same.

Underline what a young giraffe inherits from its parents.

Tell one way the young penguin is like its parents.

Young penguins are gray. Penguins become white and black as they grow.

At-Home Lab

Parent and Young
Find a picture of a young animal and its parent. Compare the two animals. Write how they are alike. Write how they are different.

Plants and Their Parents

A plant can inherit the color and shape of the parent plant. Look at the pictures. The young saguaro cactus and the adult plant are the same color. They are a similar shape too. The young cactus has spines like the adult.

A young plant can look different from its parent too. The young cactus does not have arms.

Write two things a young cactus can inherit from its parent.

A saguaro cactus does not begin to grow arms until it is about 70 years old.

This young cactus has not grown arms yet.

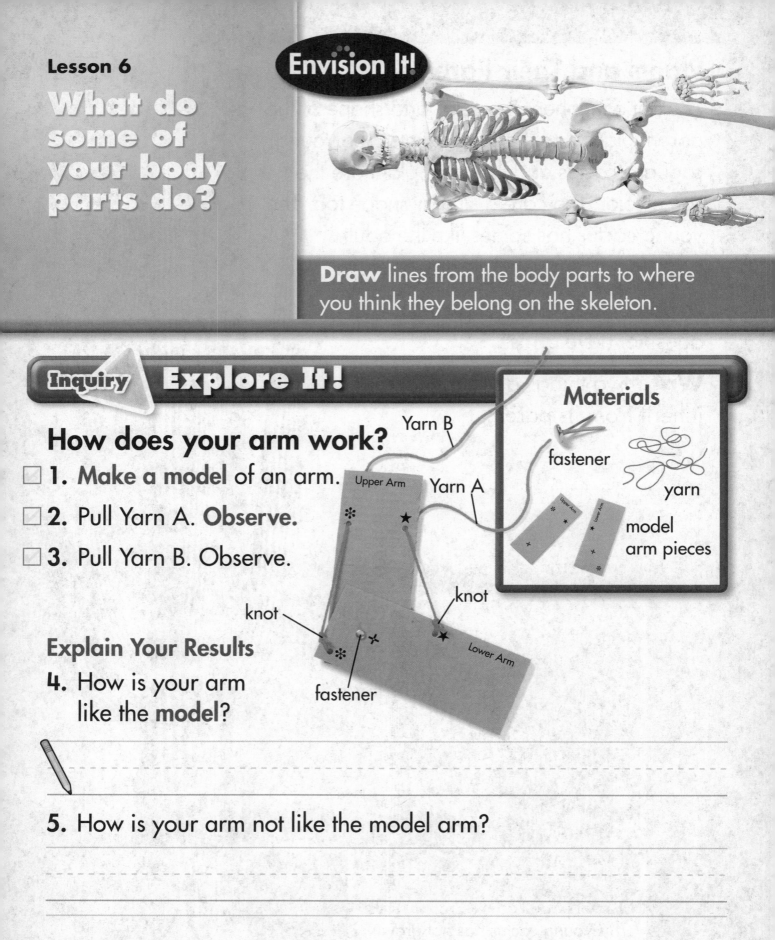

Lesson 6

What do some of your body parts do?

Draw lines from the body parts to where you think they belong on the skeleton.

Inquiry **Explore It!**

How does your arm work?

☐ 1. **Make a model** of an arm.

☐ 2. Pull Yarn A. **Observe.**

☐ 3. Pull Yarn B. Observe.

Yarn B

Yarn A

Upper Arm

knot

knot

fastener

Lower Arm

Materials

fastener

yarn

model arm pieces

Upper Arm

Lower Arm

Explain Your Results

4. How is your arm like the **model**?

5. How is your arm not like the model arm?

142

heart

brain

stomach

lungs

UNLOCK
THE BIG
?

I will know what the brain, heart, lungs, stomach, bones, and muscles do.

Word to Know

skeleton

Your Body

Think about all that your wonderful body can do. You can see, hear, run, and think! The different parts of your body work together.

Suppose a ball is coming your way. First, you see the ball. Next, you run and reach out toward the ball. Last, you catch the ball!

⊙ **Sequence Underline** the steps you take to catch the ball.

Tell how your body parts worked together.

143

Brain

Your brain is an important part of your body. Your brain controls what your body does by sending and receiving messages. Your brain helps you move, think, and feel.

You use your senses to get information. This information travels to your brain. Your brain sends messages to the other parts of your body to tell them what to do.

You hear a telephone ring. The sound travels to your brain. Your brain may tell you to answer the telephone.

You smell your favorite food. The smell travels to your brain. **Write** what your brain might tell you to do.

_____

_____

_____

Stomach

Food gives your body energy. You need energy to play and grow. Food needs to be changed before your body can use it. Your stomach helps change the food.

Muscles in your stomach mix the food. Liquids in the stomach help break the food into tiny pieces. Then the food moves out of the stomach. Other parts of the body finish changing some of your food into energy.

Draw an arrow to show how food moves from the mouth to the stomach.

Write what your stomach does.

stomach

145

Lungs and Heart

Your lungs take in air when you breathe. Oxygen is in the air. You need oxygen to live.

Your heart pumps blood to all parts of your body. Blood has materials that your body needs. Your heart pumps blood to your lungs. The blood picks up oxygen from the lungs. The blood carries the oxygen from your lungs to all parts of your body. Your heart works together with your lungs to keep you healthy.

Underline what your lungs and heart do.

Draw how your lungs would look if you were playing this instrument.

146

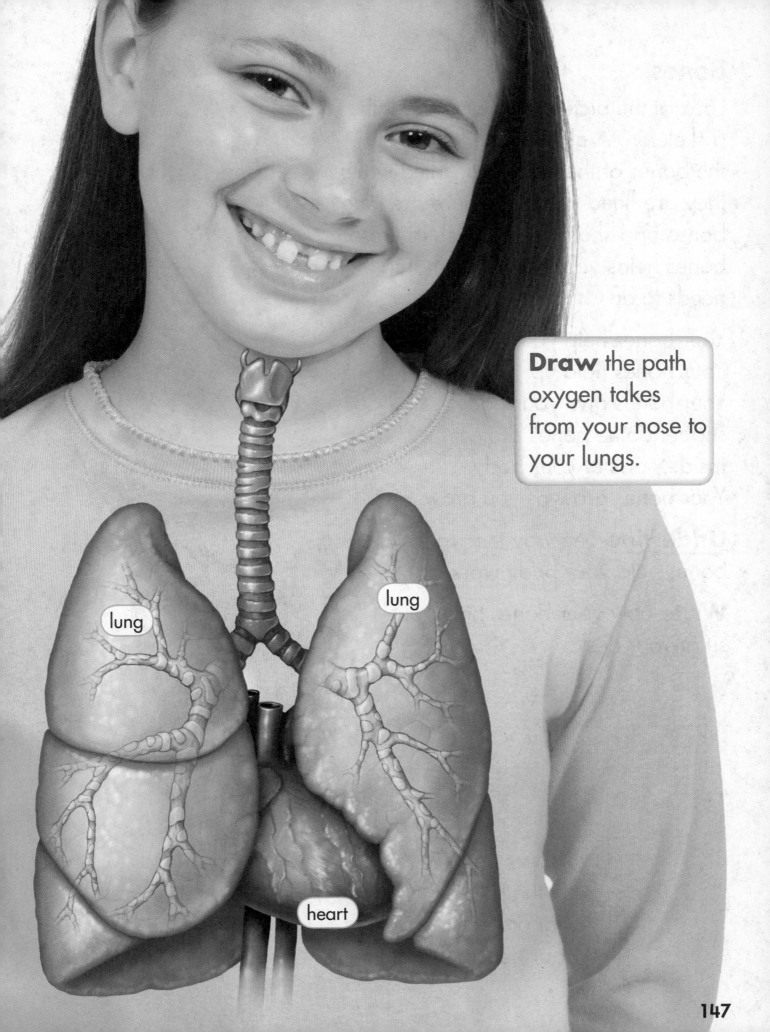

Draw the path oxygen takes from your nose to your lungs.

lung

lung

heart

147

Bones

Look at the picture of the bones. It is a skeleton. A **skeleton** is what all the bones of the body are called when they are fitted together. There are long bones and short bones. Each of these bones helps your body do what it needs to do.

Your bones help you move. Your bones hold up your body. Your bones give your body shape. Some bones protect inside parts of your body. Your bones grow as you grow.

Underline one way that your bones help your body work.

Write how your bones help you sit at your desk.

Draw an X on the bones that protect your heart.

148

Muscles

Your body has muscles. Muscles are of many different sizes and shapes.

Muscles have some of the same jobs that bones do. Muscles give your body shape. Muscles help protect some inside parts of your body too.

Your bones and muscles work together to move your body. Some muscles help you move your arms and legs. Other muscles help you open and close your eyes!

Circle the muscles you use to write in your book.

Write how your muscles help you play.

_____

_____

_____

_____

What is the life cycle of a beetle?

Follow a Procedure

☑ **1. Observe** the mealworms.

Be careful! They are alive! Handle with care.

Inquiry Skill
You **record data** when you draw what you observe.

☑ **2. Collect Data** Draw 2 stages you see.

3. Observe the mealworms for 3 weeks. Look for a new stage.

4. Draw the 3 stages.

Analyze and Conclude

5. UNLOCK THE BIG ? **Interpret Data** How did the mealworm change?

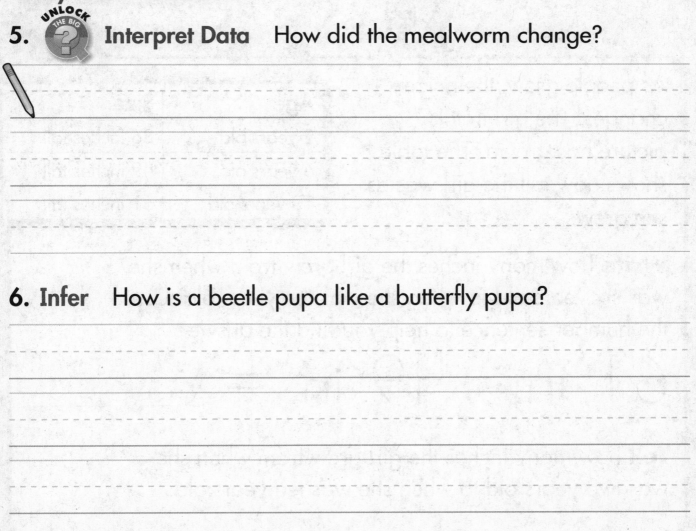

6. Infer How is a beetle pupa like a butterfly pupa?

Compare Size and Age

6 years old

2 years old

10 years old

As people grow, their size changes. The girl in this picture has grown. The table shows how tall the girl was as she grew.

Age	Size
2 years old	36 inches tall
6 years old	49 inches tall
10 years old	61 inches tall

Write how many inches the girl grew from when she was six years old to when she was ten years old. Use the number sentence to help you find the answer.

61 in. – 49 in. = _____

Tell how many inches the girl grew from when she was two years old to when she was ten years old.

Vocabulary Smart Cards

life cycle
larva
pupa
tadpole
litter
seedling
inherit
skeleton

Play a Game!

Cut out the cards.

Work with a partner to put one set of cards picture side up.

Put the other set picture side down.

Match each word with its meaning.

153

tadpole

renacuajo

life cycle

ciclo de vida

litter

camada

larva

larva

seedling

plántula

pupa

pupa

the way a living thing grows and changes

manera en que un ser vivo crece y cambia

a very young frog

una rana muy joven

a young insect

un insecto joven

all the babies born to a mammal at the same time

todos los bebés nacidos de un mamífero al mismo tiempo

stage in an insect's life between larva and adult

etapa de la vida de un insecto entre larva y adulto

a young plant

una planta joven

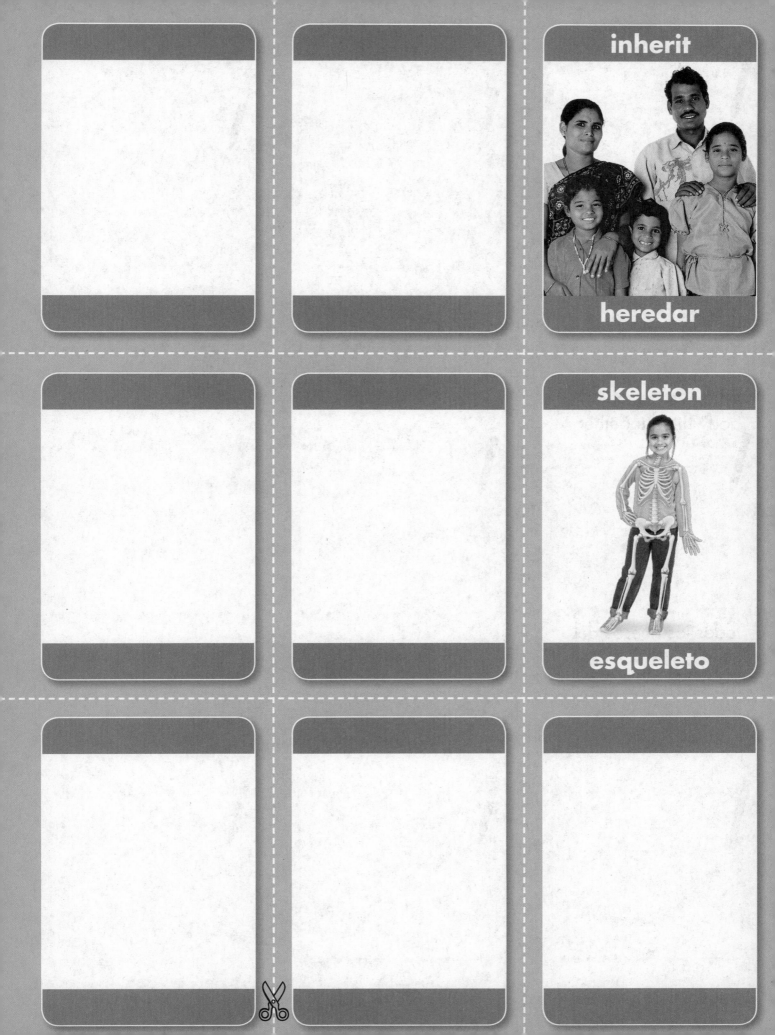

inherit

heredar

skeleton

esqueleto

to get from a parent

recibir de un
progenitor

all the bones of the
body fitted together

todos los huesos del
cuerpo juntos

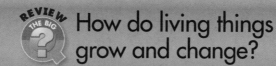

How do living things grow and change?

Life Science

Lesson 1

What is the life cycle of a butterfly?

- A butterfly's life cycle includes an egg, a larva, a pupa, and an adult.

Lesson 2

What is the life cycle of a frog?

- A frog's life cycle includes an egg, a tadpole, a young frog, and an adult frog.

Lesson 3

What is the life cycle of a mouse?

- A litter of mice are born without hair and with their eyes and ears closed.

Lesson 4

What is the life cycle of a plant?

- A bean plant's life cycle includes a seed, a seedling, and an adult.

Lesson 5

How are living things like their parents?

- Living things can inherit shape, size, and color from their parents.

Lesson 6

What do some of your body parts do?

- Your heart and lungs get oxygen to your body.
- Your skeleton gives your body shape.

Chapter Review

REVIEW THE BIG ? How do living things grow and change?

Lesson 1

1. **Vocabulary Complete** the sentence.
   The way a living thing grows and changes is called its

   _____

   _____ .

2. **Analyze Write** how a larva is different from a butterfly.

   _____

   _____

   _____

   _____

Lesson 2

⊙ 3. **Sequence Draw** an ✗ on the second stage in the life cycle of a frog.

Lesson 3

4. **Describe Write** one way a newborn mouse is different from its parents.

   _____

   _____

   _____

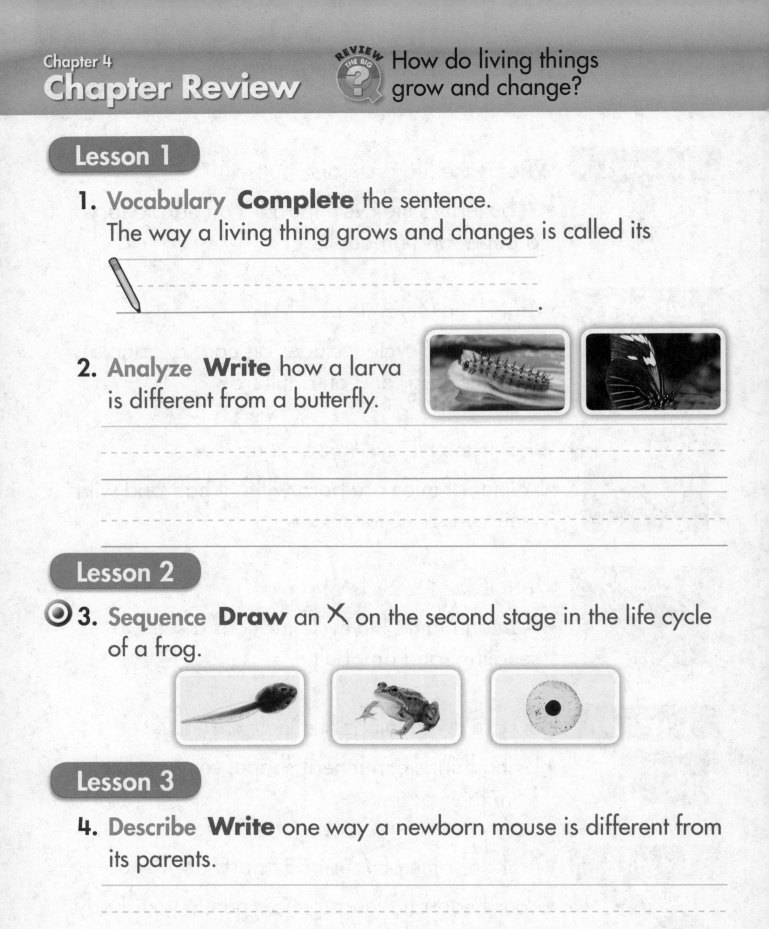

Lesson 4

5. **Vocabulary** What is the second stage in the life cycle of a bean plant? **Fill in** the bubble.

Ⓐ seed   Ⓒ seedling

Ⓑ adult   Ⓓ seed coat

Lesson 5

6. **Apply** **Write** one way a giraffe is like its parents.

_____

_____

Lesson 6

7. **Identify** (Circle) the body part that helps mix your food, break it into tiny pieces, and turn it into energy.

Got it?

⬜ **Stop!** I need help with _____

_____

▶ **Go!** Now I know _____

How can an octopus use its arms?

An octopus has suction cups on its 8 arms. It can use its arms to pick things up. The octopus can use its arms to open a jar and get a fish that is inside.

Ask a question.

How can an octopus use its arms to open a jar? Use a **model** to find out.

Make a prediction.

1. How many suction cups will you need to open a jar? Tell what you think.

I will need _____ suction cups.

Plan a fair test.

Use suction cups of the same size.

Materials

paper fish
in plastic jar
with lid

8 suction cups

Inquiry Skill
You **control
variables** when
you change
only one thing
in your test.

Design your test.

☐ **2.** List your steps.

Do your test.

☑ **3.** Follow your steps.

Collect and record data.

☑ **4.** Fill in the chart.

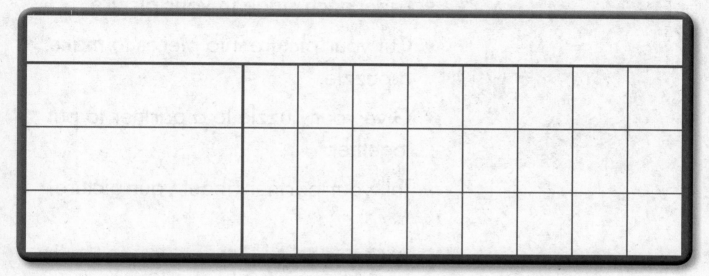

Tell your conclusion.

5. How many suction cups did you need to open the jar?

_____

_____

6. Communicate   How did you use the suction cups to open the jar?

_____

_____

_____

Performance-Based Assessment

Make a Puzzle

- Draw a picture of a butterfly life cycle on heavy paper.

- Label each stage in your picture.

- Cut your picture into pieces to make a puzzle.

- Give your puzzle to a partner to put together.

- Tell your partner about your picture.

Put On a Play

- Pretend to be an animal or plant.

- Act out things about your animal or plant and its habitat.

- Have your classmates guess what you are.

Light and Seeds

- Plant seeds in two pots.

- Provide one pot with more light.

- Draw and record the growth of each plant.

Using Scientific Methods

1. Ask a question.

2. Make a hypothesis.

3. Plan a fair test.

4. Do your test.

5. Collect and record data.

6. Draw a conclusion.

Earth Science

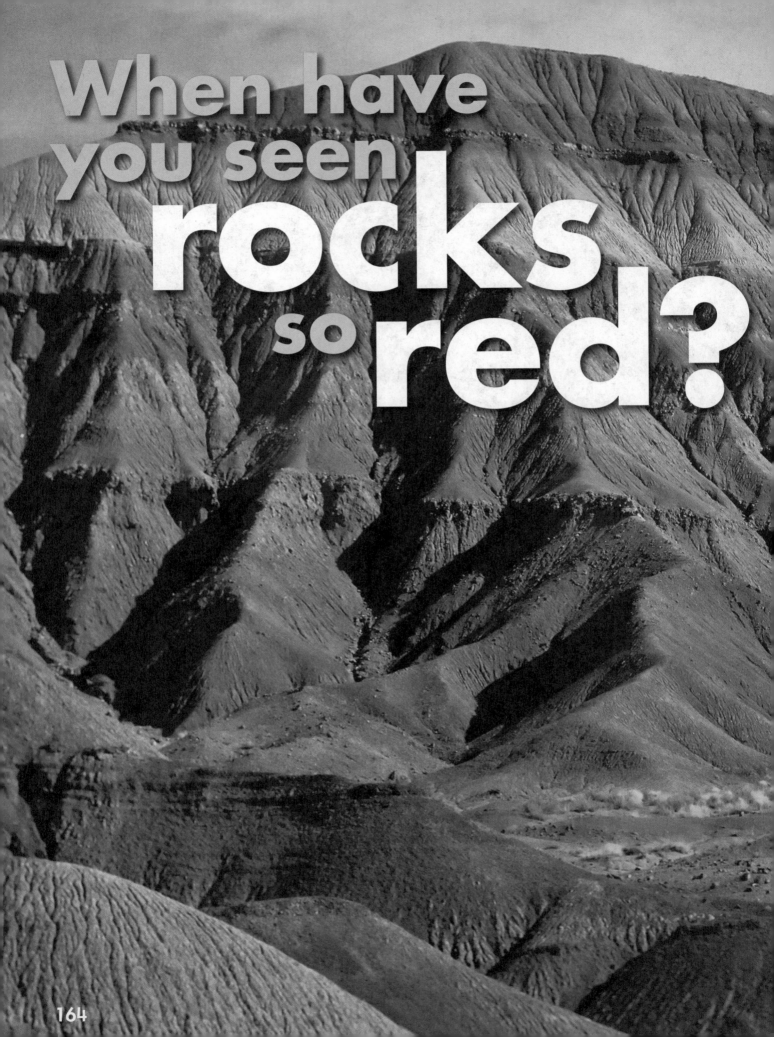

When have you seen rocks so red?

Earth's Materials

Tell how you think these rocks became this shape.

What is Earth made of?

Go to www.myscienceonline.com and click on:

UntamedScience™
Go on a science adventure with the Ecogeeks!

Got it? 60-Second Video
Take one minute to learn science!

my Planet Diary
Did you know? Find out through Planet Diary.

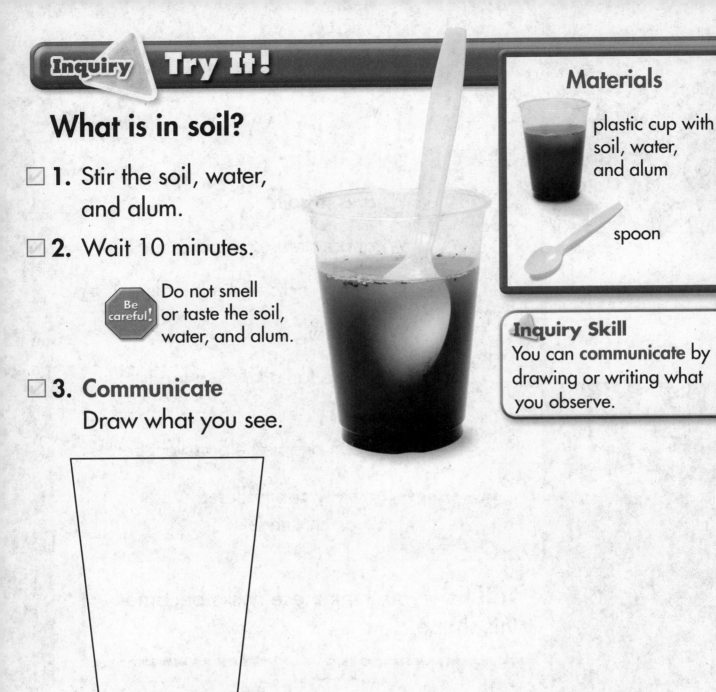

What is in soil?

☐ **1.** Stir the soil, water, and alum.

☐ **2.** Wait 10 minutes.

Be careful! Do not smell or taste the soil, water, and alum.

☐ **3. Communicate**
Draw what you see.

cup

Materials

plastic cup with soil, water, and alum

spoon

Inquiry Skill
You can **communicate** by drawing or writing what you observe.

Explain Your Results

4. Infer What do the layers tell you about soil?

_____

_____

_____

⊙ Main Idea and Details

The **main idea** is the most important idea in what you are reading. **Details** tell about the main idea.

Soil and Plants

Plants grow in many different kinds of soil. Some soils make plants grow better. Most soils hold the water that plants need. Soil gives plants materials they need to live and grow too.

Practice It!

Write two details about how soil helps plants grow.

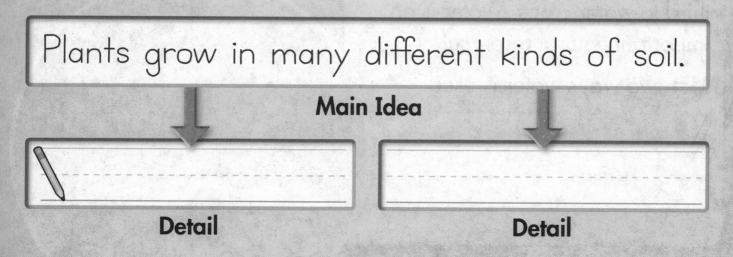

Plants grow in many different kinds of soil.

Main Idea

Detail   Detail

What are natural resources?

Tell how the trees and the cabin are connected.

my planet Diary

/// **MISCONCEPTION** ///

Read Together

People in the United States use over 400 billion gallons of water each day! We drink it. We cook with it. We use it to brush our teeth and take a bath. But that is not how most water is used. About half is used by power plants to make electricity. Farmers use another third to water crops. Water is an important natural resource!

List two ways water is used.

_____

_____

_____

The Hoover Dam power plant uses water to make electricity for people in three states.

Natural Resources

A **natural resource** is a useful material that comes from Earth. Soil, rocks, and plants are natural resources. Sunlight, water, and air are natural resources too. Living things use natural resources.

○ **Main Idea and Details**
Write the main idea.

plants

water

rocks

169

Kinds of Natural Resources

Some natural resources cannot be replaced. Oil and gas come from plants and animals that lived long ago. Oil and gas cannot be replaced. People use oil and gas for fuel. **Fuel** is anything that is used to make heat or power.

Some natural resources can be replaced. People use plants for food and clothing. They cut down trees for wood. People use wood to build things. They use wood as fuel too. People can plant new trees and other plants.

Some natural resources can never be used up. Sunlight, water, and air will never be used up. People drink water. People use water to cook and clean. Moving air is called wind. People use wind to make power.

Underline resources that cannot be replaced.

Circle resources that can be replaced.

Write three natural resources these plants need.

Draw one way this resource could be used.

Lesson 2

What are rocks and minerals?

Envision It!

Tell how these rocks are different.

Inquiry **Explore It!**

How can you sort rocks?

☐ **1.** Pour rocks and sand into the filter. Shake over the newspaper. **Observe.**

☐ **2.** Sort the rocks by size.

Materials

rocks and sand

newspaper

filter

Explain Your Results

3. You sorted the rocks by size. What is another way you could sort the rocks?

_____

- - - - - - - - - - - - - - - - - -

4. Draw a Conclusion   How does a filter help sort rocks?

_____

- - - - - - - - - - - - - - - - - -

_____

Draw your own rock.

UNLOCK THE BIG ?

I will know that Earth is made of many different kinds of rock.

Words to Know

rock
mineral

Rocks

You dig a hole in the ground. You want to find out what makes up Earth. You might find soil, sand, clay, and rocks.

Earth is made up of rocks. A **rock** is a hard, solid part of Earth. You might find rocks in your backyard, at the beach, or in a forest. Rocks are everywhere!

Roots can break rocks into smaller pieces.

◎ Main Idea and Details **Write** the main idea.

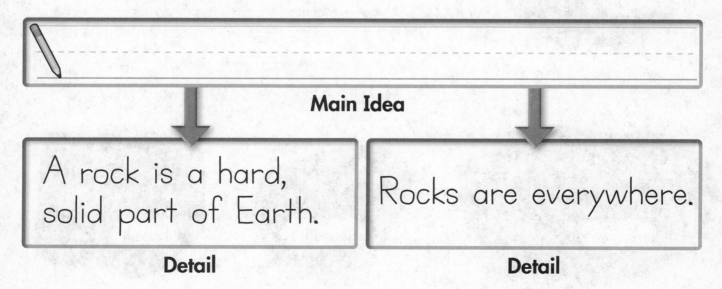

Main Idea

A rock is a hard, solid part of Earth.

Rocks are everywhere.

Detail

Detail

173

alexandrite

Many Different Rocks

Rocks can be very different. Rocks can be different colors and shapes. Some rocks are smooth. Some rocks are rough.

Rocks can be different sizes too. You can hold some rocks in your hand. They are very light. Other rocks are as big as a mountain! They are very heavy.

Look at these rocks.
Write three ways that they are different.

opal

pumice

hematite

basalt

174

Minerals

Rocks are made of minerals. A **mineral** is a nonliving material that comes from Earth. Some minerals are gold, silver, and iron. Many things are made of minerals. Some rings are made from gold. Some coins have silver in them. Some nails are made from iron.

Most rocks are made up of more than one mineral. Look at the piece of granite. Granite is a rock. Three minerals in some kinds of granite are mica, quartz, and feldspar.

Main Idea and Details
Underline three kinds of minerals named above.

mica

quartz

feldspar

granite

What is soil?

Envision It!

Tell how soil helps the flowers.

Inquiry **Explore It!**

How does soil help plants?

☐ **1.** Plant a seed in each cup.

☐ **2.** Put the cups in a sunny place.

☐ **3.** Keep the soil damp.
Add water when it is dry.

☐ **4. Observe** how the seeds grow in each soil.

Materials

clay soil   loam soil   sandy soil

3 plastic cups with soil
(1 with clay soil,
1 with loam soil,
1 with sandy soil)

3 pinto
bean seeds

water

clay soil   loam soil   sandy soil

Explain Your Results

5. **Draw a Conclusion**   In which soil did the plants grow best?

I will know how soil is formed. I will know different kinds of soil.

Words to Know

soil   loam

texture

Soil

Soil is the top layer of Earth. Soil begins to form when rocks break down into very small pieces. Small pieces of dead plants and animals are mixed in. Soil is formed.

Soil holds air and water too. Soil gets mixed when animals dig in it. Digging mixes more air and water into the soil.

Worms loosen and mix the soil.

◉ **Main Idea and Details** **Write** how soil forms.

_____

_____

_____

_____

Kinds of Soil

Different kinds of soils cover most of the land. Soils have different textures. **Texture** is how something feels.

Sandy soil is made of small pieces of rocks. Water flows through sand easily. Sandy soil can feel dry. It feels rough too.

Clay soil is made of grains that are packed together. Clay soil feels smooth. It feels soft and sticky too. The red color of some clay comes from iron in the soil. Iron is a nutrient.

Loam is a kind of soil that is made of pieces of living things that have died. It is made of sand, clay, and silt too. Silt is made of very small grains. Loam soil is black.

Look at the pictures.
Complete the sentences.

loam

Loam is made of _____, silt, clay, and pieces of living things that have died.

clay soil

Lightning Lab

Soil Survey
Look at some soil. Do not touch the soil. Write the color. Tell about the size of the grains in the soil.

The nutrient _____ makes the clay soil red.

sandy soil

Sandy soil feels _____.

179

Soil and Plants

Different kinds of plants grow best in different kinds of soil.

Sandy soil is not good for many plants. It does not hold water well.

Clay soil holds water better than sandy soil. It is packed tightly together. Some plants do not grow well in it. Their roots cannot push through the soil to grow.

Loam is the best soil for growing most kinds of plants. It holds water well. Plants are able to get the water they need to grow.

Look at the pictures.
Complete the sentences.

Write why you think sandy soil does not hold water well.

180

is best for growing most plants.

does not hold water well.

is packed tightly together.

What are some kinds of land and water?

Tell what kinds of land and water you see.

MY PLANET DIARY

Connections

A chain of mountains is called a mountain range. The Rocky Mountains form the longest mountain range in North America. Only the Andes Mountains in South America form a longer mountain range.

These are not the longest mountain ranges on Earth, though. The longest mountain range is under the ocean! It is four times longer than the Rockies, Andes, and Himalayas put together.

Tell what you think the land under the ocean looks like.

Rocky Mountains

Words to Know

landform
glacier

Land and Water

What is Earth's surface like? Over two-thirds of Earth's surface is covered by water. Most of this water is in the ocean. Soil and plants cover much of the rest of Earth's surface. Rock is found beneath the water, soil, and plants.

◉ **Main Idea and Details**
Describe what covers most of Earth's surface.

ocean

land

183

Landforms

Earth's surface has many different landforms. A **landform** is a natural feature on Earth. Landforms are different sizes and shapes.

Mountains, hills, and valleys are landforms. Mountains and hills are raised parts of Earth's surface. A mountain is very high and large. A hill is not as high as a mountain. A valley is the low land between mountains or hills.

Plains and islands are landforms too. A plain is a large, flat area of land. An island is land that is surrounded by water.

⊙ **Main Idea and Details** <u>**Underline**</u> the sentence that tells what a landform is.

Look at the pictures.
Complete the sentences.

At-Home Lab

Compare Landforms
Choose two landforms. Draw a picture of each landform. Write one way the landforms are alike. Write one way the landforms are different.

A mountain is very _____ _____ .

Draw an X on a hill.
Circle a valley.

A plain is a _____ _____ _____ area of land.

_____ _____ surrounds an island.

185

The Ocean

Earth has different bodies of water. The ocean is the largest body of water. It covers most of Earth. The ocean has different parts. The Pacific Ocean is one part. The Atlantic Ocean is another part. All of the parts of the ocean are connected.

Ocean water is salty. People cannot drink salt water.

Tell why you think people cannot drink ocean water.

Lakes and Ponds

Lakes are much smaller than the ocean. Ponds are much smaller than lakes. Lakes and ponds form when water fills low places on land.

Most lakes and ponds are fresh water. People can drink fresh water.

Complete the sentence.
A lake forms when water fills

Rivers and Streams

Rivers and streams form when water runs downhill. Small streams join together to form rivers. Most rivers flow into lakes or into the ocean. Most rivers and streams are fresh water.

Complete the sentence.
A river forms when water runs

_____
_ _ _ _ _ _ _ _ _ _ _ _ _ _ _ _ _ _ _ _
_____ .

Glaciers

Glaciers form in very cold places. A **glacier** is a large body of moving ice. Glaciers move very slowly. Most of Earth's fresh water is frozen into glaciers. People cannot drink the frozen water.

Write one way that glaciers are like rivers and streams.

_____
_ _ _ _ _ _ _ _ _ _ _ _ _ _ _ _ _ _ _ _
_____

187

How can people help protect Earth?

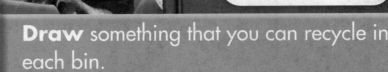
Envision It!

PAPER

Draw something that you can recycle in each bin.

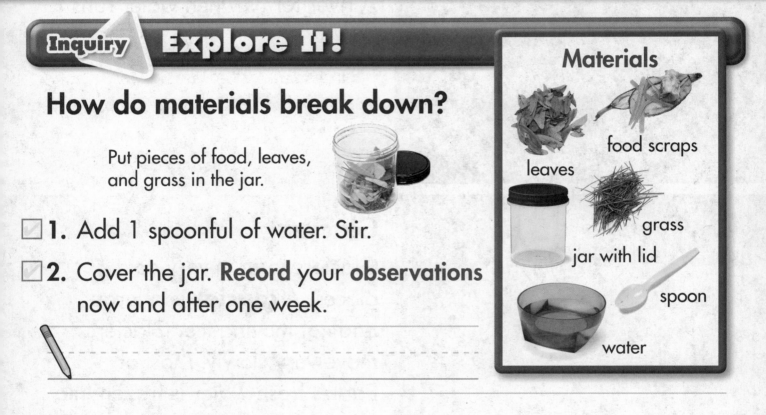

Inquiry **Explore It!**

How do materials break down?

Put pieces of food, leaves, and grass in the jar.

☐ **1.** Add 1 spoonful of water. Stir.

☐ **2.** Cover the jar. **Record** your **observations** now and after one week.

Materials

leaves

food scraps

grass

jar with lid

spoon

water

Explain Your Results

3. Infer Composting gets important materials back to the soil. How does this help the environment?

METAL   PLASTIC

Words to Know

pollution   refuge
recycle

Pollution

Sometimes Earth changes because of pollution. **Pollution** happens when something harmful is added to the land, air, or water. Pollution can harm people and other living things in the environment. The environment is everything around living things.

Many people work together to help the environment. They pick up trash. They help clean up polluted lakes, rivers, and oceans. They walk or ride bikes. This helps keep the air clean.

Underline the sentence that tells what pollution can do.

Tell how people can help the environment.

Reduce and Reuse

All of the things people use come from Earth. The metal in a paper clip comes from rocks. Paper comes from trees.

People can protect Earth by reducing the amount of things they use. Reduce means to use less. How can you reduce the amount of water you use? You can turn off the water while brushing your teeth.

People can reuse things too. Reuse means to use again. You can reuse paper by writing on both sides.

Tell a partner how reusing paper helps protect Earth.

Tell what you could reuse to make the musical instrument in the picture.

Go Green

New Uses for Old Cans
Make a container out of an old can. Make sure the can is clean. Decorate the can. Use it to hold pencils or pens.

Recycle

People can recycle. **Recycle** means to change something so it can be used again. Paper, plastic, metal, and glass can be recycled. Some parts of this playground are made from recycled plastic milk containers.

Write what the boy in the picture is doing to take care of Earth.

_____

_____

_____

Protecting Plants and Animals

How can people keep plants and animals safe? They can take care of plant and animal habitats.

Trees are cut down for wood. A forest habitat changes when trees are cut down. Some animals might lose their homes.

People can help protect forest habitats. People can plant trees to replace the ones that are cut down. Animals can make their homes in the new trees.

Draw an animal that might lose its habitat when trees are cut down.

New trees can be homes for animals.

Tell a partner how you could help the animal find a new habitat.

A Safe Place

People build homes, stores, and factories. They build roads and parking lots. Plants and animals that lived in the trees and on the land may have no place to go.

People can take plants and animals to a refuge. A **refuge** is a safe place to live. People cannot build on land that is used as a refuge.

Write how a refuge helps protect animals.

_____

_____

_____

Look at the picture. **Tell** how learning about animals could help protect them.

People can see plants and animals at a refuge.

193

Investigate It!

How can "polluted" water be cleaned?

Follow a Procedure

☐ **1.** Stir the "polluted" water. **Observe** the polluted water and tap water with the hand lens. **Record** your observations.

☐ **2.** Wait 5 minutes. Record your observations of the polluted water.

☐ **3.** Pour the polluted water into the filter. Do not pour out mud.

☐ **4.** Pour the filtered water into the cup. Observe.

Materials

"polluted" water (prepared by teacher)

tap water

timer or stopwatch

hand lens

tape

plastic cup

filter assembly (prepared by teacher)

spoon

Inquiry Skill You infer when you get ideas from what you know.

Be careful! Do not drink the water!

Data Table

Type of Water	Observations
"Polluted" Water	
Tap Water	
Polluted Water (After 5 Minutes)	
Filtered Water	

Analyze and Conclude

5. What happened when the polluted water sat for 5 minutes?

_____

_____

_____

6. Infer Why might the filtered water be unsafe to drink?

_____

_____

_____

_____

Collecting Rocks

You can go rock collecting where you live. Go to your backyard or a nearby park. Look around. Find as many different kinds of rocks as you can.

Try to find different sizes and shapes of rocks. Try to find rough and smooth rocks. Try to find many different colors of rocks.

Ask an adult to go with you!

Write how many rocks you found.

Draw and **color** the rocks you collected.

Vocabulary Smart Cards

natural
  resource
fuel
rock
mineral
soil
texture
loam
landform
glacier
pollution
recycle
refuge

Play a Game!

Cut out the cards. Choose a card and give your partner clues. Have your partner guess the word.

mineral

mineral

natural resource

recurso natural

soil

suelo

fuel

combustible

texture

textura

rock

roca

a useful material that comes from Earth

un material útil que proviene de la Tierra

a nonliving material that comes from Earth

un material sin vida que viene de la Tierra

anything that is burned to make heat or power

cualquier cosa que se quema para que dé calor o energía

the top layer of Earth

la capa superior de la Tierra

a hard, solid part of Earth that is not soil or metal

una parte dura y sólida de la Tierra que no es suelo o metal

how something feels

cómo se siente algo al tacto

198

pollution

contaminación

loam

marga

recycle

reciclar

landform

accidente
geográfico

refuge

refugio

glacier

glaciar

soil that is made of sand, silt, clay, and pieces of living things that have died

suelo formado por arena, cieno, arcilla y pedazos de cosas vivas que han muerto

something harmful added to land, air, or water

algo dañino que se desecha en la tierra, el aire o el agua

a natural feature on Earth

formación natural en la Tierra

to change something so it can be used again

cambiar algo de manera que se pueda usar otra vez

a large body of moving ice

gran masa de hielo que se mueve

a safe place to live

lugar seguro para vivir

Chapter 5
Study Guide
REVIEW THE BIG ? What is Earth made of?

Earth Science

Lesson 1

What are natural resources?

• Soil, water, and air are natural resources.
• Fuel is burned to make heat or power.

Lesson 2

What are rocks and minerals?

• Rocks are made up of minerals.
• Minerals are materials that come from Earth.

Lesson 3

What is soil?

• Sandy soil, clay soil, and loam have different textures.

Lesson 4

What are some kinds of land and water?

• Mountains and plains are landforms.
• Rivers and glaciers are kinds of water.

Lesson 5

How can people protect Earth?

• People recycle to reduce pollution.
• Animals can find a safe home in a refuge.

Lesson 1

1. Vocabulary List three natural resources.

_____

- - - - - - - - - - - - - - - - -

_____

- - - - - - - - - - - - - - - - -

_____

2. Classify Which natural resource cannot be replaced?
Fill in the bubble.

Ⓐ sunlight   Ⓒ oil

Ⓑ air   Ⓓ water

Lesson 2

◉ **3. Main Ideas and Details Read** the paragraph below.
Underline two details.

Diamonds are the hardest minerals on Earth.
Diamonds can scratch glass. However, they can be
broken with a hammer.

4. Compare Look at the rocks.
Write two ways they are
alike.

_____

- - - - - - - - - - - - - - - - -

_____

Lesson 3

5. Identify (Circle) the picture of sandy soil.

Lesson 4

6. Apply Write two ways an ocean and a lake are different.

_____
_____
_____
_____

Lesson 5

7. Describe Write one way people can protect Earth.

_____
_____
_____

Got it?

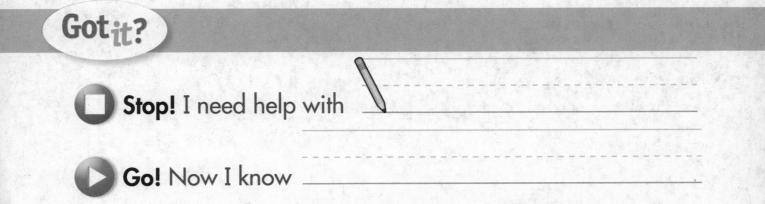

☐ **Stop!** I need help with _____
_____

▶ **Go!** Now I know _____

What can you see in the night sky?

The Solar System

Chapter 6

Try It! How does the sun's movement cause shadows to change?

Lesson 1 What is the sun?

Lesson 2 What are the moon and stars?

Lesson 3 What is the solar system?

Investigate It! How can you make a model of a constellation?

Tell why you think some stars are brighter than others.

THE BIG ? What are the sun, moon, and planets like?

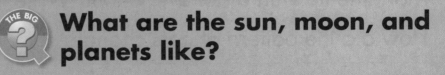

Go to www.myscienceonline.com and click on: ⊗

UntamedScience™
Watch the Ecogeeks in this wild video.

Got it? ⏱ 60-Second Video
Watch and learn.

Science Songs
Sing along with animated science songs!

Explore It! Animation
Explore what can happen in a new way.

How does the sun's movement cause shadows to change?

☐ **1.** Glue the Sun Tracker to cardboard.

☐ **2.** Put a piece of clay on the Sun Tracker. Put a stir stick in the clay.

☐ **3.** Put the Sun Tracker outside in the sun.

Point the paper North. Your teacher will tell you which way is North.

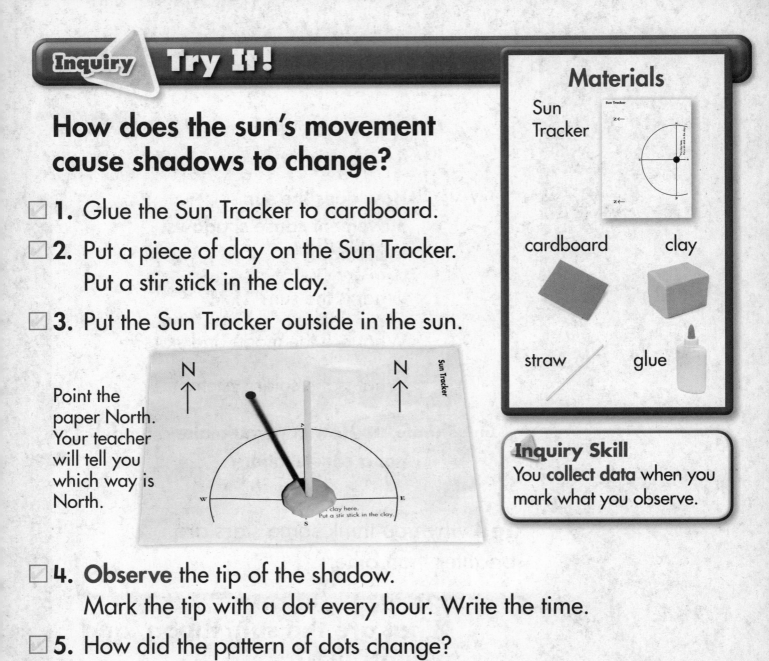

☐ **4.** **Observe** the tip of the shadow. Mark the tip with a dot every hour. Write the time.

☐ **5.** How did the pattern of dots change?

Materials

Sun Tracker

cardboard   clay

straw   glue

Inquiry Skill
You **collect data** when you mark what you observe.

Explain Your Results

6. Infer How can you use a shadow to predict the sun's position?

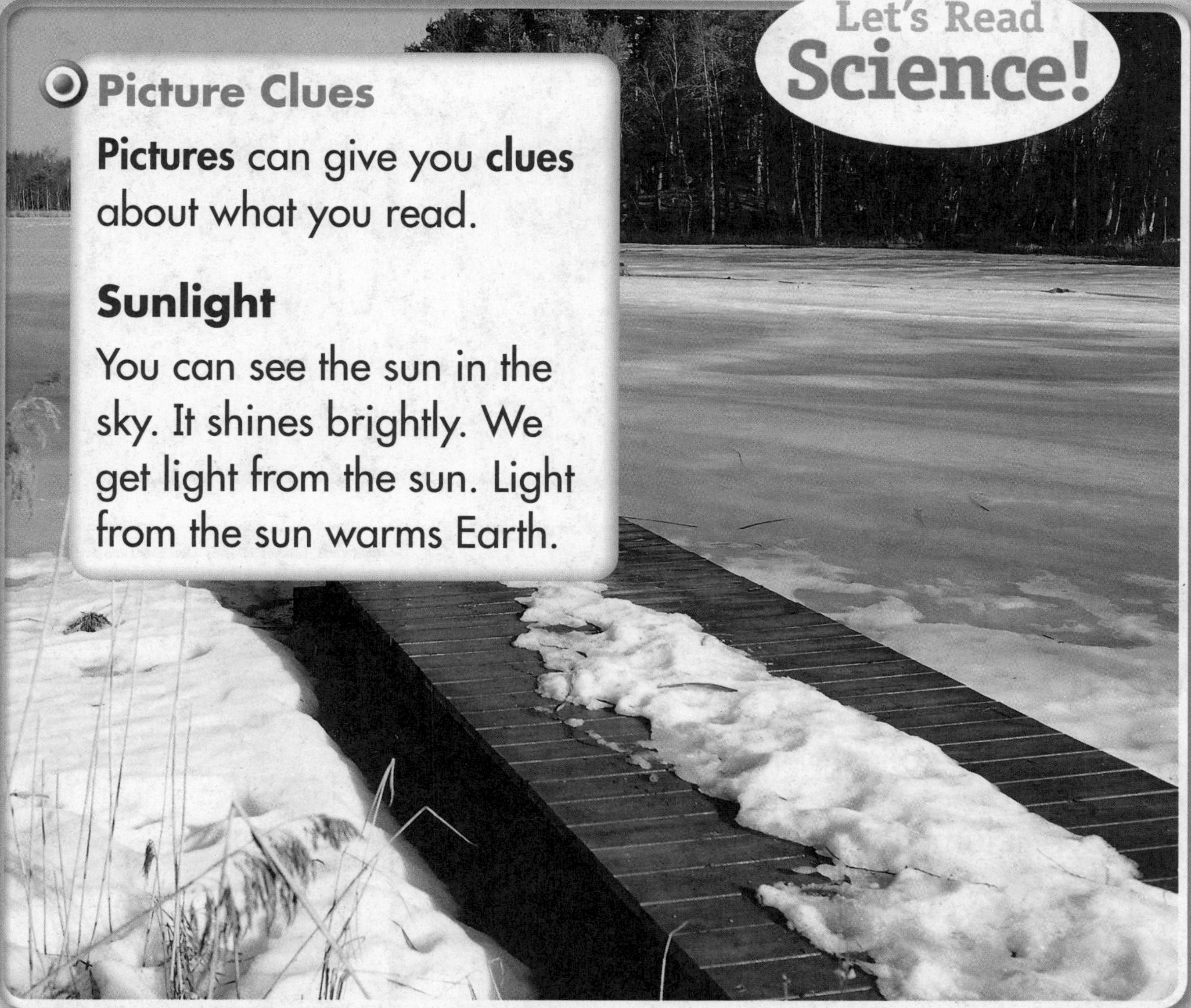

Picture Clues

Pictures can give you **clues** about what you read.

Sunlight

You can see the sun in the sky. It shines brightly. We get light from the sun. Light from the sun warms Earth.

Practice It!

Look at the picture. **Write** how you know sunlight can melt snow.

Sunlight can melt snow.

Clue

Clue

What is the sun?

Envision It!

Tell what you think makes the sand on this beach warm.

Inquiry **Explore It!**

What can the sun's energy do?

- [ ] 1. Tilt a solar collector toward the sun.

- [ ] 2. Place a lump of clay near the bowl. Put a crayon into the clay.

- [ ] 3. **Observe** both crayons after 10 minutes. Describe both crayons.

Materials

solar collector with crayon

clay

unwrapped crayon

timer or stopwatch

book

Explain Your Results

4. **Infer**   Explain your **observation.**

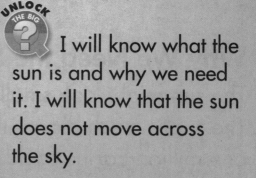

I will know what the sun is and why we need it. I will know that the sun does not move across the sky.

Word to Know

sun

The Sun

The **sun** is a star. It is made of hot, glowing gases. The sun looks like a bright, yellow ball in the sky.

The sun seems brighter and larger than other stars. This is because the sun is the closest star to Earth. The sun is so bright that you cannot see other stars during the day.

Tell about the shape and color of the sun.

This is what the sun looks like in space.

Why We Need the Sun

The sun might look small, but it is very big. The sun is much bigger than Earth. About one million Earths could fit inside the sun!

The sun is important to Earth. Earth gets light from the sun. Light is one kind of energy. Light energy causes heat. Most living things on Earth need light and heat. You can live on Earth because of light and heat from the sun.

Write why the sun is important to you.

sun

Look at the pictures below.
Tell how you know the sun is giving off light.

At-Home Lab

Shade and Sun
Sit outside in a shady spot. Close your eyes. Count to one hundred. Open your eyes. Move to a sunny spot. What feels different when you sit in the sunlight? What looks different?

The sun's heat keeps people warm.

Geckos sit in the sun to warm their bodies.

Plants need sunlight to grow.

Earth

Sun in the Sky

The sun seems to move across the sky during the day. The sun looks low in the sky in the morning at sunrise. The sun is high in the sky at noon. It looks low in the sky again in the evening at sunset.

Label each picture. Write the words sunrise, noon, or sunset.

The sun does not really move across the sky. Earth moves. Each day, Earth spins around once. As Earth spins, the sun seems to be moving.

You may not see the sun on a cloudy day. The sun is behind the clouds. The sun always shines, even when you cannot see it.

What are the moon and stars?

Envision It!

Use a white crayon. **Trace** the dotted lines to see a star pattern.

Inquiry Explore It!

How does the shape of the moon appear to change?

Materials

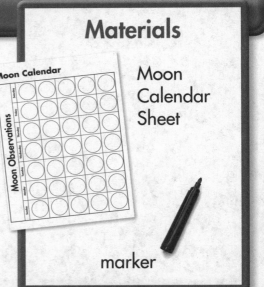

Moon Calendar Sheet

marker

☐ **1.** Use a Moon Calendar.

☐ **2.** Observe the moon every night.

☐ **3.** **Record data** by drawing pictures on the calendar.

Explain Your Results

4. Communicate Describe how the moon appears to change.

Tell a partner what the pattern looks like.

Words to Know

star   crater
constellation   phase

The Night Sky

Your part of Earth faces away from the sun at night. You can see stars in the sky. A **star** is a ball of burning gases that gives off light and heat. The stars are different colors. They are different sizes. Most stars look small because they are so far away.

The moon is much smaller than a star. But the moon is closer to Earth. So the moon looks bigger in the night sky.

Compare the size of the moon and the stars.

_____

_____

_____

You can see stars and the moon in the night sky.

215

Constellations

Long ago, people saw shapes in some groups of stars. They connected the stars with imaginary lines to form pictures. A group of stars that forms a picture is a **constellation.** Many constellations are named for animals or people.

Constellations can look like different things to different people. People long ago thought the constellation called Leo looked like a lion. What does it look like to you?

_____

_ _ _ _ _ _ _ _ _ _ _ _ _ _ _ _ _ _

_____

This constellation looks like a lion. It is called Leo.

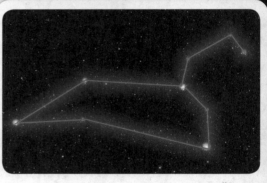

This constellation looks like a hunter holding a club. It is called Orion.

The Moon

The moon looks like the biggest and brightest object in the night sky. The moon does not make its own light. It reflects light from the sun.

The moon is round like Earth. The moon is much smaller than Earth. The moon is made of rock. It has mountains and deep craters. A **crater** is a hole in the ground shaped like a bowl.

Describe the moon.
Draw an X on a crater.

A crater forms when a large rock from space hits the moon.

Moon at Night

The moon moves in a path around Earth. It takes about four weeks for the moon to go once around Earth. The moon seems to change shape as it moves.

Sometimes the moon looks round. This is called a full moon. Sometimes you see smaller parts of the moon. Sometimes you cannot see the moon at all.

Sometimes you can see the moon during the day. However, it is harder to notice when the sun is out.

Look at the pictures of the moon.
Draw an X on the full moon.

Phases of the Moon

Why does the shape of the moon seem to change? Remember that the moon reflects light from the sun. You only see the part of the moon that has light shining on it. The shape of the lighted part of the moon is called a **phase.**

Write why the moon seems to change shape.

At-Home Lab

The Big Dipper

People name groups of stars. One group is called the Big Dipper. Go out at night with an adult. Find the Big Dipper. Tell why it is called the Big Dipper.

It takes about a month to see all of the phases of the moon.

What is the solar system?

Draw an X on the sun. **Circle** Earth.

my planet diary Did You Know?

Read Together

Scientists once considered our solar system to have nine planets. Pluto was the ninth planet. Pluto is very small. It is even smaller than Earth's moon. In 2006, scientists decided that Pluto is too small to be a planet. It is now known as a dwarf planet. Many dwarf planets are called plutoids in honor of Pluto.

Why did scientists decide Pluto should not be a planet?

Pluto

Words to Know

solar system

The Sun and the Planets

You live on Earth. Earth is a planet. A planet is a large, round body of rock or gas that moves around the sun. This movement is called an orbit. An orbit is a path around another object. Other planets orbit the sun too.

◉ **Picture Clues Look** at the picture. **Write** about the planets that orbit the sun.

| Planets orbit the sun. |

↓ ↓

Clue   **Clue**

The Solar System

The sun, the planets and their moons, and other objects that move around the sun make up the **solar system.** The sun is the center of our solar system. All of the objects in the solar system orbit the sun.

Each planet takes a different length of time to orbit the sun. Mercury takes about 88 days to orbit the sun. Earth takes about 365 days. Neptune takes about 60,190 days. That is almost 165 Earth years!

sun

Mercury

Venus

Earth

Mars

Jupiter

Circle the planet closest to the sun.
Draw an X on the planet that is farthest from the sun.
Write why you think it takes Neptune longer than Earth to orbit the sun.

Lightning Lab

Order Planets
Work as a group. Write the names of the eight planets and the sun on index cards. Have each group member select a card. Line up in the order of the sun and planets in the solar system.

Saturn

Uranus

Neptune

How can you make a model of a constellation?

Follow a Procedure

☐ **1. Make a model** of a constellation. Poke holes through paper.

Materials

safety goggles

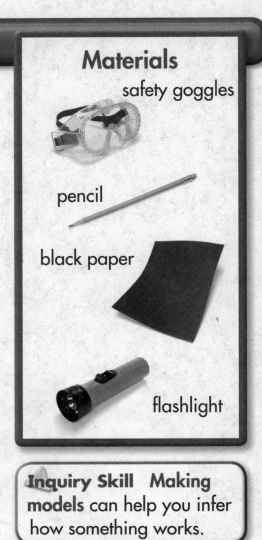

pencil

black paper

flashlight

Inquiry Skill Making models can help you infer how something works.

☐ **2.** Hold the paper near a wall in a dark room.

☐ **3.** Shine a flashlight through the paper. **Observe.**

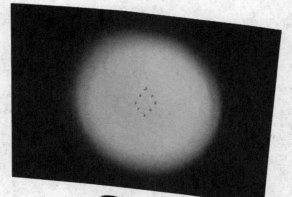

☐ **4. Record.** Draw your constellation.

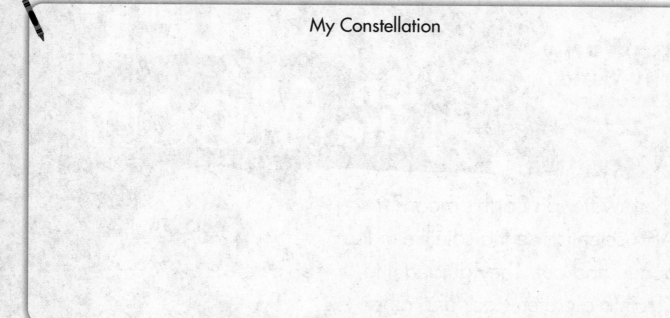

My Constellation

Analyze and Conclude

5. How is your **model** like a real constellation?

_____

- -

_____

- -

_____

6. Infer How is your model different from a real constellation?

_____

- -

_____

- -

_____

Water on the Moon

Is there water on Earth's moon? NASA scientists sent a satellite to the moon to find out. They guided it to crash into a crater. Rock and other material shot up from the moon's surface. The scientists found signs of water in the material.

This is an important discovery. It helps us understand the moon better. It may help future moon explorers too. People need water. But water is hard to carry into space. Finding water on the moon could solve the problem!

You need water. People working on the moon need water too.

Write why water on the moon is an important discovery.

Vocabulary Smart Cards

sun
star
constellation
crater
phase
solar system

Play a Game!

Cut out the cards.

Pick a card.

Think of a sentence that uses the word. Say the sentence to a partner.

Have your partner tell the definition of the word.

crater
cráter

sun
Sol

phase
fase

star
estrella

solar system
sistema solar

constellation
constelación

the closest star to
Earth

la estrella más
cercana a la Tierra

a hole in the ground
shaped like a bowl

hueco con forma
de tazón que se
encuentra en la tierra

a ball of burning
gases that gives off
light and heat

bola de gases muy
calientes que produce
calor y luz

the shape of the
lighted part of the
moon

forma de la parte
iluminada de la Luna

a group of stars that
forms a picture

grupo de estrellas que
forman una figura

the sun, the planets
and their moons, and
other objects that
move around the sun

el Sol, los planetas
con sus satélites y
otros objetos que
giran alrededor del
Sol

Study Guide

What are the sun, moon, and planets like?

Earth Science

Lesson 1

What is the sun?

- The sun is a star made of hot, glowing gases.
- The sun gives off light and heat.

Lesson 2

What are the moon and stars?

- Groups of stars form constellations.
- We can observe the moon's craters and phases.

Lesson 3

What is the solar system?

- The planets and their moons and other objects in the solar system move around the sun.

Chapter Review

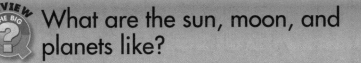

What are the sun, moon, and planets like?

Lesson 1

1. **Classify** (Circle) the picture of the sun's position in the sky at sunrise.

2. **Apply Write** what warms the sidewalk on a bright day.

_____

_____

_____

Lesson 2

3. **Vocabulary** What is the shape of the lighted part of the moon called? **Fill in** the bubble.

   Ⓐ crater   Ⓒ constellation
   Ⓑ phase   Ⓓ star

4. **Describe Write** two ways the stars and the moon are different.

   _____

   _____

   _____

   _____

230

Lesson 3

5. Vocabulary **Complete** the sentence.

The sun, the planets and their moons, and other objects

_____

make up the _____ .

6. Picture Clues **Look** at the picture.
Name the three planets
that are closest to the sun.

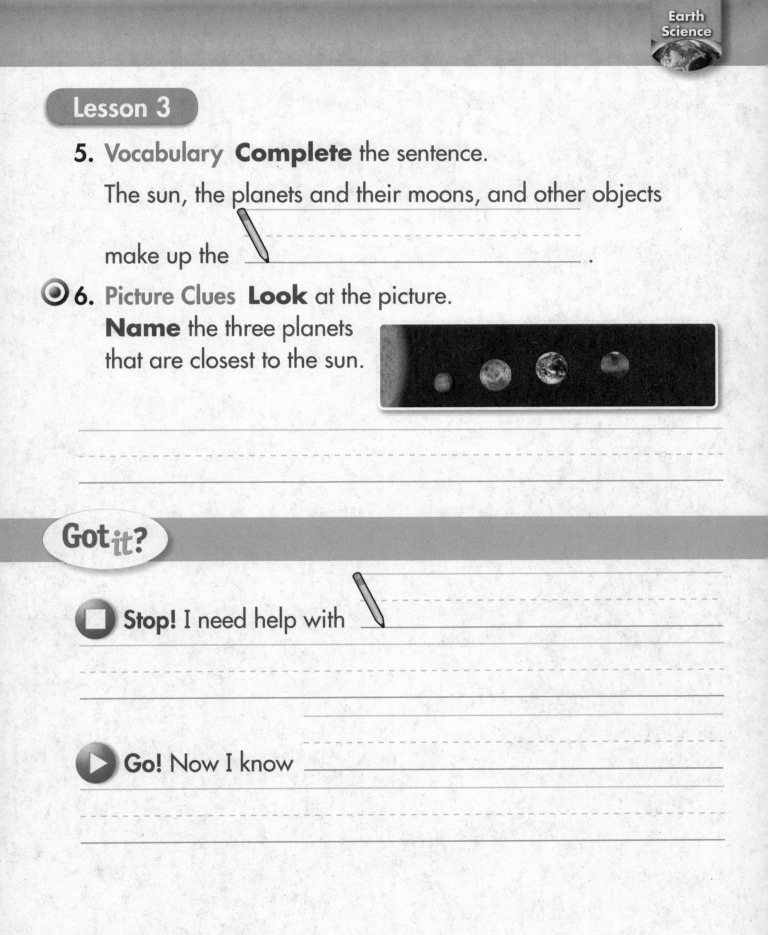

_____

_____

_____

Got it?

☐ **Stop!** I need help with _____

_____

_____

▶ **Go!** Now I know _____

_____

_____

When can you see a rainbow?

Weather

Try It! How can you show the temperature?

Investigate It! What is your weather like?

Chapter 7

Tell what the weather is like when you can see a rainbow.

? **How does weather change over time?**

Go to www.myscienceonline.com and click on:

UntamedScience™
Watch the Ecogeeks in this wild video.

Got it? 60-Second Video
Watch and learn.

Envision It!
Interact with science to find out what you know.

Vocabulary Smart Cards
Mix and match vocabulary practice!

233

How can you show the temperature?

☐ **1.** Use the Thermometer Model. Put each end of your yarn through the holes in front of your model.

☐ **2.** Your teacher will tell you the temperature. Move the yarn up or down to show the temperature.

☐ **3.** Use a real thermometer. **Measure** the temperature outside. **Record** on the Thermometer Chart.

☐ **4.** Repeat for 3 more days.

Explain Your Results

5. Tell about the changes in temperature you **measured.**

_____
- - - - - - - - - - - - - - - - - - - -
_____
- - - - - - - - - - - - - - - - - - - -
_____
_____

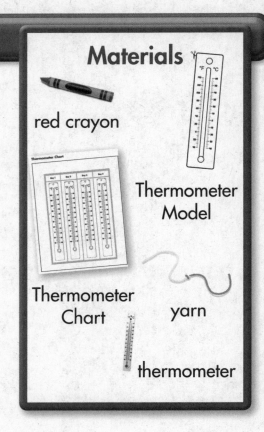

Materials

red crayon

Thermometer Model

Thermometer Chart

yarn

thermometer

> **Inquiry Skill** You can use a thermometer to **measure** temperature.

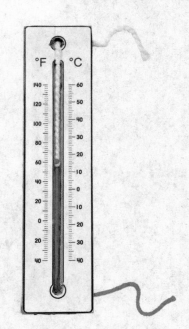

Compare and Contrast

Compare means to tell how things are alike. **Contrast** means to tell how things are different.

Spring and Winter

Spring can be warm. Spring can be windy. Spring is sometimes very rainy. Winter can be cold. Winter can be windy. Winter can be snowy too.

Practice It!

Compare and **contrast** spring and winter.

Compare	Contrast

What is the water cycle?

Write what you think will happen to the puddle.

MY PLANET DIARY

Did You Know?

Read Together

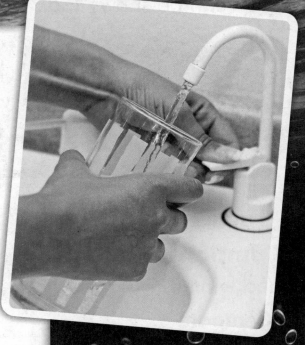

Rain and melted snow flow into lakes and other bodies of water. We get drinking water from some of these places. Did you know that we also get drinking water from under the ground?

Water from rain and snow soaks into the ground. It fills up spaces between rocks. We drink this water too.

What happens to water that soaks into the ground? **Underline** the sentence that tells you.

Words to Know

water cycle

Clouds in the Sky

Rain falls from clouds in the sky. Clouds are made of tiny drops of water and ice.

The water in clouds comes from Earth's surface. It comes from oceans, rivers, and lakes. The sun warms the water. The water rises into the air.

⊙ **Main Idea and Details** **Write** another detail that goes with the main idea.

clouds

ocean

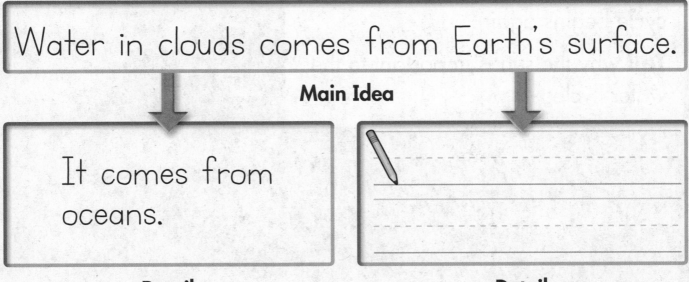

Water in clouds comes from Earth's surface.

Main Idea

It comes from oceans.

Detail

Detail

The Water Cycle

The way water moves from Earth to the clouds and back to Earth again is called the **water cycle.**

The sun warms the water on Earth. Some of the water evaporates, or changes into a gas. The gas is called water vapor. Water vapor rises into the air.

Water vapor in the air condenses when it gets cold. Condense means to change from a gas into a liquid. Water vapor changes into tiny drops of water. These drops form clouds.

Water falls from clouds. It flows into rivers, lakes, and oceans. The sun warms the water, and the water cycle begins again.

Tell why the sun is important to the water cycle.

Water falls from clouds as rain or snow.

Water flows into rivers, lakes, and oceans.

Water vapor condenses and forms clouds.

Water changes into water vapor. The water vapor rises into the air.

Lightning Lab

Measure Evaporation
Use a paper cup and water. Plan an activity that shows evaporation.

239

How can you describe weather?

Tell what the weather is like in the picture.

Inquiry **Explore It!**

Which way does the wind blow?

☐ **1.** Label the plate **N, E, S,** and **W.** Add clay.

☐ **2.** Tape the tissue to the straw. Put the straw in the clay.

☐ **3. Observe** outside. What direction is the wind coming from?

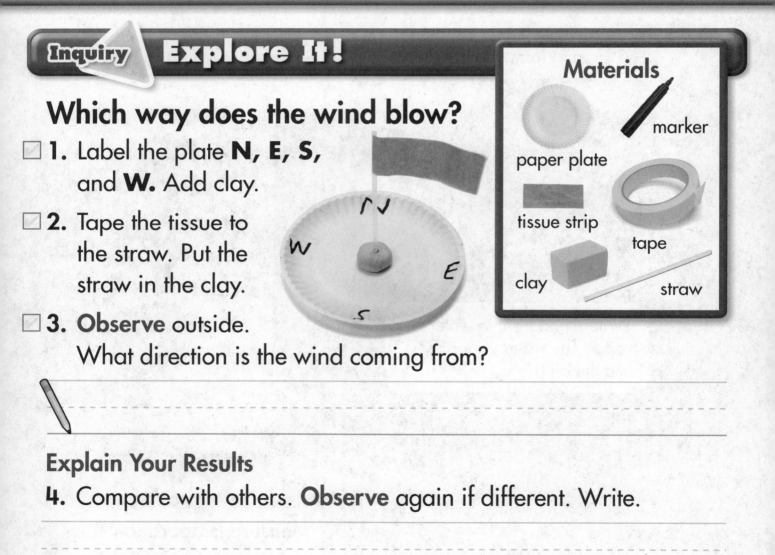

Materials

marker

paper plate

tissue strip

tape

clay

straw

_____

- -

_____

Explain Your Results

4. Compare with others. **Observe** again if different. Write.

_____

- -

_____

_____

UNLOCK THE BIG I will know how to describe different kinds of weather.

Words to Know

temperature
precipitation

Weather

You wake up in the morning. How do you know what to wear? Check the weather! Weather is what the air outside is like.

Sometimes you can guess the weather by looking outside. You can also look in a newspaper or on a Web site. These sources tell if the weather will be wet or dry. They tell the air temperature too. **Temperature** is how hot or cold something is. The sun changes the air temperature.

Tell how the sun affects weather.

◉ **Picture Clues Look** at this weather information from a Web site. (Circle) the day that might be rainy. **Draw** an X on the day that will be hottest.

Weather Forecast

Monday
26° C
(79° F)

Tuesday
24° C
(75° F)

Wednesday
21° C
(70° F)

241

Wet Weather

Wet weather happens when water falls from clouds. The water that falls to Earth is called **precipitation.** Snow, rain, sleet, and hail are kinds of precipitation. Snow falls when the air is cold. Rain falls in warmer weather. Sleet is rain that turns to ice as it falls.

Draw what might fall from clouds when the sun warms the air.

At-Home Lab

Make a List
Write what you can do on a sunny day. Write what you can do on a rainy day. Tell how the weather affects what you can do for fun.

Spring rains help plants grow.

Dry Weather

Most places have some wet weather and some dry weather. A drought is one kind of dry weather. A drought can happen when a place has much less wet weather than usual. There may not be enough water for many living things during a drought.

Tell how the ground looks in a drought.

Some places have more dry weather than wet weather.

How can you measure weather?

Envision It!

The wind makes the windsock move.

Inquiry **Explore It!**

How much rain falls?

Make a rain gauge.

Materials

masking tape

plastic jar

metric ruler

☐ **1.** Make twelve lines 1 cm apart on a piece of tape.

☐ **2.** Number the lines.

☐ **3.** Fasten the tape to the jar.

☐ **4.** Make a plan to **observe** your rain gauge.

Explain Your Results

5. Communicate How could you use your rain gauge to find how much rain falls?

_____

_____

_____

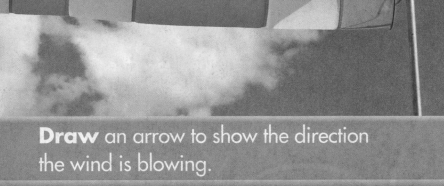

Draw an arrow to show the direction the wind is blowing.

Word to Know

wind

Why We Measure Weather

Suppose there is a storm outside. What might you see? You might see trees moving in the wind. **Wind** is moving air. You know the wind is blowing. But you cannot tell how fast it is moving.

Scientists measure weather for many different reasons. Sometimes they measure weather to warn people about storms. An anemometer is a tool that measures the speed of wind. It helps scientists know when winds are dangerous.

Tell what kind of weather the picture shows.

◉ **Main Idea and Details** **Read** the second paragraph. **Underline** the sentence that tells the main idea.

245

Tools for Measuring Weather

Tools help scientists study weather. Scientists use tools to measure temperature, wind, and rainfall.

A wind vane shows the direction of the wind. The wind vane points to where the wind is coming from.

A rain gauge measures how much rain has fallen. Raindrops fall into the gauge. Numbers tell the amount of rain in inches and centimeters.

A thermometer measures temperature. This thermometer shows the temperature in degrees Celsius and Fahrenheit.

Picture Clues What temperature is shown on the thermometer?

246

Predict Weather

Scientists gather weather information over many years. They learn what the weather of a place might be like at different times. They use this information to predict weather.

The graph shows rainfall for Baton Rouge, Louisiana. It tells how much rain fell in March over three years.

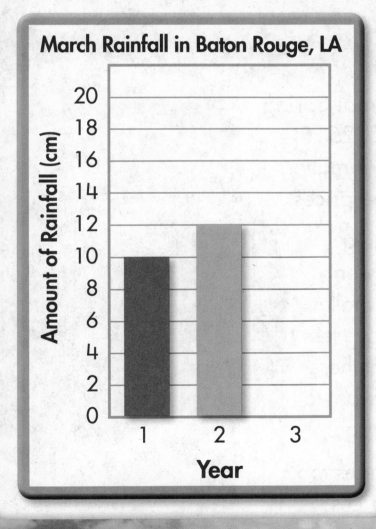

March Rainfall in Baton Rouge, LA

At-Home Lab

Chart the Weather
Chart the weather for a week. Look at the weather report in the newspaper every day. Record the temperature. Put a thermometer outside. Check it every day at the same time. Compare the temperature information from both sources.

Draw a bar on the graph to show that it rained 10 centimeters in Year 3.

Tell which year had the most rainfall. How much fell?

How does weather change?

Envision It!

spring

summer

Color the trees to show what they look like in each season.

MY PLANET DIARY

FunFact

Read Together

Freezing weather strikes Alabama! Spring temperatures drop below −4° C (25° F). Why should this matter to you? It matters because weather can affect food prices.

Alabama grows peaches. Freezing temperatures can hurt peach flower buds. Damaged buds produce smaller fruit or no fruit at all. Farmers have less good fruit to sell. This means that there are fewer peaches than people want to buy. When this happens, prices go up!

Freezing weather can hurt oranges too. How might this affect orange prices?

_____

_____

fall

winter

Word to Know

pattern

Weather Patterns

Weather follows a pattern. A **pattern** is the way something repeats itself.

Weather follows patterns from day to day. In many places, the temperature is cool in the morning. It is warmer in the afternoon. Often the temperature gets cool again at night. The amount of change differs from place to place and from day to day.

On a January day, the temperature might change by 28° F in Denver, Colorado. It might change by only 14° F in Boston, Massachusetts.

⊙ **Compare and Contrast Write** how daily temperature patterns might be the same and different in two places.

Compare

Contrast

249

Spring and Summer

Weather follows patterns from season to season. The seasons are spring, summer, fall, and winter. The seasons repeat every year.

Some spring days are cool. Some are warm. Spring days can be rainy. Buds and leaves begin to grow on plants during spring. Birds and other animals have babies.

Summer comes after spring. Some summer days are hot. The nights are often warm. Trees and other plants have lots of green leaves. Flowers bloom and many fruits and vegetables grow.

⊙ **Compare and Contrast Tell** how temperature and precipitation in spring and summer are different where you live.

spring

summer

fall

winter

Fall and Winter

Fall comes after summer. Some fall days are warm. Some are cool. Many plants stop growing. Leaves change color and drop from some trees. Many animals store food for the coming winter.

Winter comes after fall. Winter in some places can be very cold and snowy. Water in ponds and lakes may freeze. Many trees have no leaves at all. Some animals hibernate, or sleep, all winter long.

Compare and Contrast Tell how fall and winter are different.

Lightning Lab

Changing Seasons
Make a chart. Name a season. Write three words that tell about the weather of your season. Tell what the weather is like before the season. Tell what the weather is like after the season.

How can you stay safe in severe weather?

Envision It!

Tell what you think you should do if you see lightning.

Inquiry **Explore It!**

What do tornadoes look like?

☑ **1. Make a Model** Put the tops of the bottles together. Seal with duct tape.

← duct tape

☑ **2.** Flip the bottles. The water is now on top.

☑ **3.** Swirl. **Observe** the top bottle.

Explain Your Results

4. How is your **model** like a tornado? How is it different?

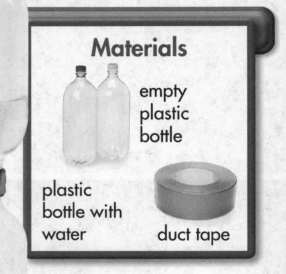

Materials

empty plastic bottle

plastic bottle with water

duct tape

Words to Know

severe weather

Thunderstorms

A thunderstorm is one kind of severe weather. **Severe weather** is dangerous weather. A thunderstorm is heavy rain with thunder and lightning. Sometimes thunderstorms have hail and strong winds too.

Underline two details about thunderstorms.

Hail is pieces of ice that fall from clouds.

Thunderstorm Safety

• Find shelter in a sturdy building.

• Keep away from windows, water, and trees.

• Keep away from metal objects.

• Keep away from things that use electricity.

253

Tornadoes

Tornadoes can happen during thunderstorms. A tornado is a small but very strong wind that comes down from thunderstorm clouds.

Tornadoes form very quickly. It is hard to predict when tornadoes will happen. A tornado can destroy things in its path.

Write why it is important to be ready for severe weather.

_____

_____

_____

_____

Tornado Safety

- Go to the basement or an inside room.

- Crouch under the stairs or near an inner wall.

- Stay away from windows.

- Cover your head.

Draw an X on the place where the tornado in this picture came down from.

At-Home Lab

Safe Places
Work with an adult. Identify one kind of severe weather. Make a plan to stay safe. Tell where safe places are. Tell what things you will need.

Hurricanes

A hurricane is a large storm that starts over warm ocean water. A hurricane has heavy rains. The rains can cause floods. A hurricane has very strong winds. The winds can knock down trees and buildings.

Compare and Contrast **Write** how tornadoes and hurricanes are alike and different.

_____

_____

_____

_____

_____

_____

Hurricane Safety

- Move away from the ocean.
- Bring loose objects inside.
- Stay inside and away from windows.
- Store extra food and water in your home.

Draw an arrow to show which way the wind is blowing.

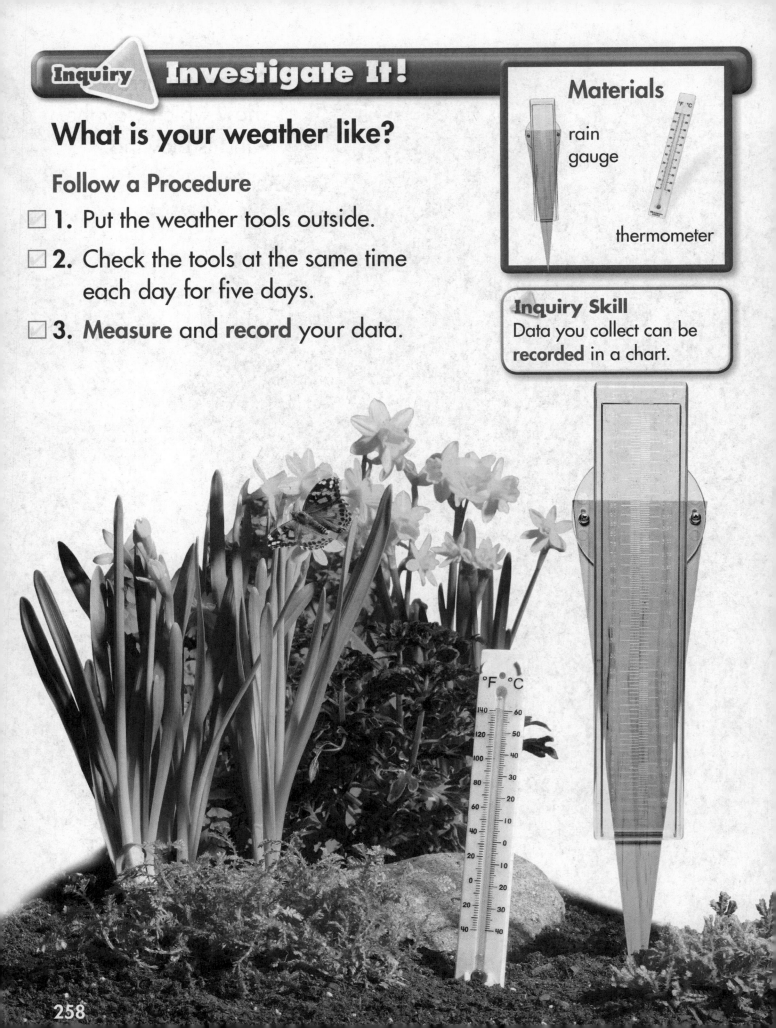

What is your weather like?

Follow a Procedure

☐ **1.** Put the weather tools outside.

☐ **2.** Check the tools at the same time each day for five days.

☐ **3.** **Measure** and **record** your data.

Materials

rain gauge

thermometer

Inquiry Skill
Data you collect can be **recorded** in a chart.

Rain and Temperature Observations

Day of the Week	Rain (cm)	Temperature (°C)
Monday		
Tuesday		
Wednesday		
Thursday		
Friday		

Analyze and Conclude

4. **Classify** the days as rainy or not rainy.

Rainy _____

Not Rainy _____

5. Tell about the temperature over the five days.

_____

_____

6. Tell how the weather changed over the five days.

_____

_____

_____

NATIONAL Hurricane Center

Hurricanes are very dangerous. People need time to prepare. Scientists at the National Hurricane Center help people prepare. They watch weather patterns so that they can warn people about approaching hurricanes.

Scientists use computers and other technology to track hurricanes.

The National Hurricane Center is in Miami, Florida. Miami is sometimes hit by hurricanes. The Center is prepared. The building can survive hurricane winds!

Tell how watching weather patterns might help scientists protect people.

Vocabulary Smart Cards

water cycle
temperature
precipitation
wind
pattern
severe
    weather

Play a Game!

Cut out the cards.

Work with a group.

Pick a card.

Tape a card to the back of each group member.

Have everyone guess his or her word.

wind

viento

water cycle

ciclo del agua

pattern

patrón

temperature

26° C
(79° F)

temperatura

severe weather

tiempo severo

precipitation

precipitación

the way water moves
from Earth to the
clouds and back to
Earth again

manera en que se
mueve el agua de la
Tierra hacia las nubes
y de nuevo a la Tierra

moving air

aire que se mueve

how hot or cold
something is

cuán caliente o fría
está una cosa

the way something
repeats itself

la manera en que
algo se repite

the water that falls to
Earth

el agua que cae a la
Tierra

dangerous weather

tiempo peligroso

Study Guide

 How does weather change over time?

Lesson 1

What is the water cycle?

- The sun warms water in the water cycle.
- Water vapor condenses to make clouds.

Lesson 2

How can you describe weather?

- Weather can be wet or dry.
- Temperature is how hot or cold something is.

Lesson 3

How can you measure weather?

- Scientists use tools to measure weather.
- Wind is moving air.

Lesson 4

How does weather change?

- Weather can follow a pattern from day to day and from year to year.

Lesson 5

How can you stay safe in severe weather?

- You can make a plan to stay safe in severe weather.

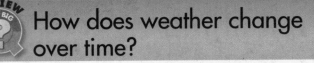
Lesson 1

1. **Think** about the water cycle. What happens to water vapor in the air when it gets cold? **Fill in** the bubble.

   Ⓐ It evaporates.   Ⓒ It condenses.

   Ⓑ It melts.   Ⓓ It boils.

2. **Analyze Draw** what is missing in this picture.

Lesson 2

3. **Vocabulary Look** at the weather information below from a Web site. **Circle** the temperature.

Wednesday

16° C
(61° F)

4. **Describe** What causes a drought?

_____

Earth
Science

Lesson 3

5. Classify Draw an **X** on the tool that measures temperature.

Lesson 4

◎ **6. Compare and Contrast Write** how spring and fall are different.

_____

Lesson 5

7. Identify Draw a line from the picture to the word that goes with it.   lightning   tornado   hurricane

Got it?

☐ **Stop!** I need help with _____

▶ **Go!** Now I know _____

Does gravel, sand, or soil make the best imprint?

Materials

safety goggles

pencil

3 index cards

3 paper plates

plastic cup with gravel

plastic cup with soil

plastic cup with sand

shell

Inquiry Skill
In a fair test you change only one thing.

Sometimes sand slowly changes to rock. An imprint made by a plant or animal can become a fossil in the rock.

Ask a question.

Which will make the best imprint?

Make a prediction.

1. What makes the best imprint?
   The best imprint will be made in
   (a) gravel.
   (b) sand.
   (c) soil.

Plan a fair test.

Use the same amount of gravel, sand, and soil.

Design your test.

☑ **2.** Draw how you will set up your test.

☑ **3.** List your steps.

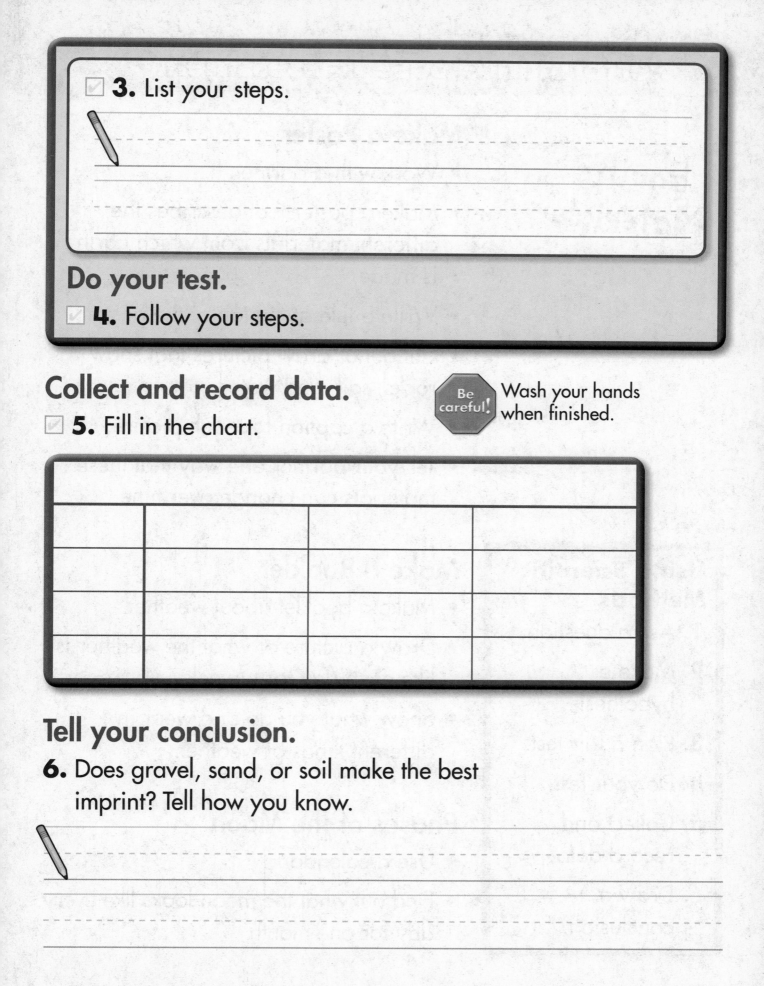

Do your test.

☑ **4.** Follow your steps.

Collect and record data.

☑ **5.** Fill in the chart.

Be careful! Wash your hands when finished.

Tell your conclusion.

6. Does gravel, sand, or soil make the best imprint? Tell how you know.

Earth's Materials

Make a Poster

- Work with a partner.
- Make a poster that describes the different materials from which Earth is made.
- Write a title at the top of the poster.
- Cut out or draw pictures that show rocks, soil, and water.
- Write a caption for each picture.
- Tell your partner one way that these materials can change over time.

Using Scientific Methods

1. Ask a question.
2. Make a hypothesis.
3. Plan a fair test.
4. Do your test.
5. Collect and record data.
6. Draw a conclusion.

Make a Booklet

- Make a booklet about weather.
- Draw a picture of what the weather is like each day for a week.
- Show what you do and wear in different kinds of weather.

Phases of the Moon

- Use a calendar.
- Find out what the moon looks like every day for one month.

Physical Science

How high can they fly?

Matter

Try It! What affects evaporation?

Lesson 1 What are some properties of matter?

Lesson 2 What are solids, liquids, and gases?

Lesson 3 What are some ways matter can change?

Lesson 4 How can water change?

Investigate It! How can properties change?

Tell what you think makes these balloons fly.

What is matter?

Go to www.myscienceonline.com and click on:

Untamed Science
Ecogeeks answer your questions.

Got it? 60-Second Video
Take one minute to learn science!

Envision It!
See what you already know about science.

Science Songs
Sing along with animated science songs!

What affects evaporation?

Evaporation is changing a liquid to a gas.

☑ **1.** Put a lid on one cup.

☑ **2.** Draw a line to show the water level.

☑ **3. Collect Data**   Each day draw a line to show the water level.

Materials

2 plastic cups half full of water

marker

1 lid

Inquiry Skill You collect data when you record what you observe.

water level in open cup

lid—
water level in covered cup

Explain Your Results

4. Communicate   What happened to the water level in each cup?

_____

_____

_____

5. Explain any differences in group results.

_____

_____

_____

_____

Draw Conclusions

You **draw conclusions** when you decide about something you see or read.

A Hot Day

You are playing outside on a hot day. You bring a glass of ice water with you to drink. After a while, you notice that the ice is gone.

Practice It!

Write what you think happened to the ice.

I know

It is a hot day.

My conclusion

What are some properties of matter?

Envision It!

Circle the orange that sank.

Materials

marker

plastic bag

penny

foil

pencil

Inquiry **Explore It!**

How can you classify matter?

☐ 1. **Classify** the objects as metal or nonmetal.

☐ 2. Find something that is metal and bendable.

_____

Explain Your Results

3. **Infer** Are all metal objects bendable? Explain.

_____

_____

4. What is another way to classify the objects?

_____

_____

I will know that matter has many different properties.

Words to Know

matter
property
thermometer

Draw one object that you think will float.

Matter

Everything you see around you is made of matter. **Matter** is anything that takes up space and has mass. Mass is the amount of matter in an object. Objects that have a lot of matter are heavy. The car in the picture is heavy. Objects that do not have a lot of matter are light. The bicycle is light.

Some things you cannot see are made of matter. The air around you has matter.

The cars and the bike are made of matter.

⊙ **Draw Conclusions** **Write** a conclusion about the mass of a car.

I know

A car has a lot of matter.

My conclusion

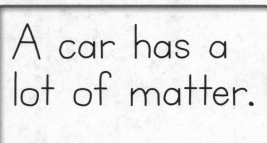

Properties of Matter

Different kinds of matter have different properties. A **property** is something about an object that you can observe with your senses. You can describe matter by telling about its properties. Weight is a property of matter. Weight is how heavy or light something is.

Find an object in your classroom.
Tell its color.
Measure its weight. **Use** a scale.

The tape is sticky.

At-Home Lab

Describe Materials
Observe objects made of paper, metal, plastic, rock, and wood. Record the materials used in each object. Record its texture, color, and shape.

Color and Texture

Color is a property of matter. Matter can be brown, purple, blue, or any other color you can think of.

Texture is a property of matter. Texture is how something feels. Objects can feel smooth or rough. The top of a table is smooth. A dry sponge is rough.

Find a yellow object in the picture. **Tell** about its texture.

These pipe cleaners are red, yellow, and green.

Shape and Size

Shape is a property of matter. Matter can be different shapes such as round, flat, or square.

Size is a property of matter too. Matter can be big or small. Matter can be long or short.

You can use tools to measure the size of objects. You can use a ruler to measure small objects. You can use a meterstick to measure large objects.

Draw an X on two objects you would measure with a ruler.

ruler

(Circle) two objects you would measure with a meterstick.

meterstick

Measure the length of the picture of the picnic blanket in centimeters.

_____ cm

Sink or Float

Whether an object sinks or floats is a property of matter.

The golf ball sinks to the bottom of the vase. The table-tennis ball floats at the top of the vase.

Look at the picture of the vase. **Draw** another object that you think will sink.

Circle the object below that you think will float.

Temperature

Temperature is a property of matter. It tells how hot or cold something is.

A **thermometer** is a tool that measures temperature. A thermometer can measure the temperature of the air. The red liquid in the thermometer below goes up when it is getting warmer. The red liquid goes down when it is getting colder. The number next to the top of the red liquid is the temperature.

Fill in the thermometer below to show how 5° Celsius (41°F) would look.

Write the difference in temperature between the two thermometers.

This thermometer shows that it is 30° Celsius (86°F).

What are solids, liquids, and gases?

Envision It!

Circle three solids. **Draw** an X on three liquids.

my planet diary Did You Know?

Read Together

What makes a thermometer work? It works because of the properties of liquids. A liquid takes up less space when it is cooled. It takes up more space when it is heated.

The liquid inside most thermometers is either alcohol or mercury. The liquid goes up in the tube when it is warmed. It goes down when it is cooled.

It has to be very, very cold for alcohol or mercury to freeze. Water freezes at 32° F. **Write** why water would not work in a thermometer.

_____

_____

_____

UNLOCK THE BIG ? I will know that matter can be a solid, a liquid, or a gas.

Words to Know

solid
liquid
gas

Solids

Everything around you is made of matter. Three states of matter are solid, liquid, and gas.

A **solid** is matter that keeps its own size and shape. Solids take up space and have weight. Look at the picture. Each object in the box keeps its own size and shape.

Underline three states of matter.

This art box and the objects in it are solids.

Draw one more solid that might go in the art box.

283

Liquids

Liquid is matter that does not have its own shape. Liquids take the shape of their containers.

Water is a liquid. Suppose you pour water into a jar. The water will take the same shape as the jar.

Look at the picture. Suppose you pour water into the funnel. The water changes shape in the funnel.

The water changes shape again in the tube. Then the water takes the shape of the different containers.

Write how solids and liquids are different.

_____

_____

_____

_____

_____

At-Home Lab

Water and Ice
Put some ice cubes in a bowl. Fill the bowl with water. Tell what happened to the solids. Tell what happened to the liquid.

Look at the picture.
Draw two shapes the water takes.

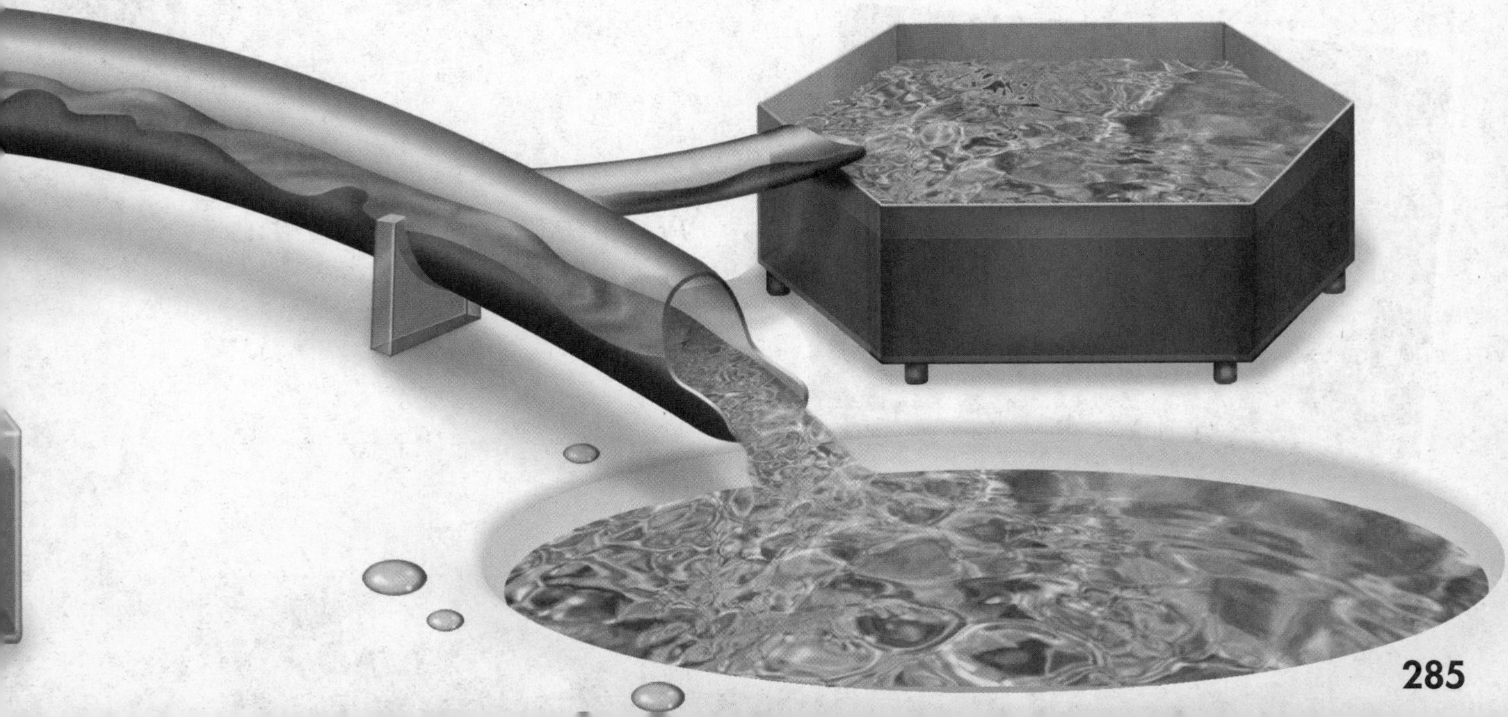

285

Gases

Gas is matter that does not have its own size or shape. Gas takes the size and shape of what it is in. Gas takes up all of the space inside its container. The bubbles in the picture are filled with gas.

You know that air is all around you. Air is made of gases that you cannot see.

How are liquids and gases alike?

_____

- - - - - - - - - - - - - - - - -

_____

_____

- - - - - - - - - - - - - - - - -

_____

Where is the gas in this bouncer?

_____

- - - - - - - - - - - - - - - - -

_____

- - - - - - - - - - - - - - - - -

Draw an arrow to the gas in a bubble.

Tell what shape the gas takes.

What are some ways matter can change?

Envision It!

Tell how the balloons were changed.

Inquiry **Explore It!**

How can you change clay?

☐ **1.** Make a ball of clay.
Squeeze it. **Record** what happens.

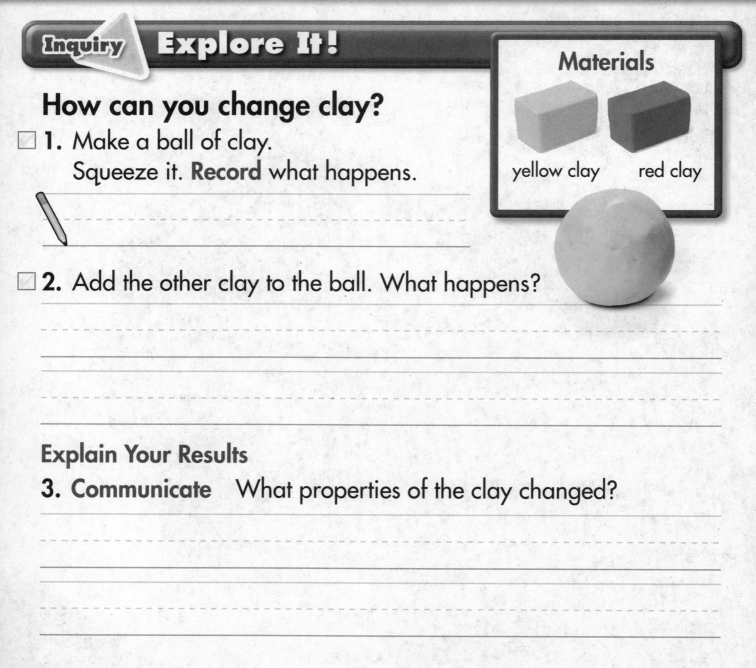

Materials

yellow clay   red clay

☐ **2.** Add the other clay to the ball. What happens?

Explain Your Results

3. Communicate   What properties of the clay changed?

UNLOCK THE BIG ? I will know that matter can be changed in many ways.

Words to Know

physical change
mixture
evaporate

Changing Matter

Matter can be changed. A **physical change** happens when matter changes but does not become a new kind of matter.

You can cut paper with scissors. Cutting causes a physical change. Cutting changes the size and shape of paper. But it is still paper after you cut it.

You can sharpen a pencil to change its size and shape. Sharpening causes a physical change. It is still a pencil after you sharpen it.

What is another physical change you can make to a pencil?

_____

_____

_____

289

Mold It, Fold It, Tear It, Bend It

Matter can be changed in other ways too. Matter can be molded, folded, torn, and bent.

Different matter changes in different ways. Suppose you pull clay apart. You can put clay back together. Suppose you tear paper. You cannot put paper back together.

Draw the clay and pipe cleaners after they have changed.

Clay can be molded into a new shape.

Paper can be torn to change its size.

Other Ways Matter Can Change

Some changes are not physical changes. Sometimes matter can be changed completely. Baking bread dough in an oven will change it. The dough is changed into something different. Baked bread cannot be changed back into dough. The bread comes out of the oven warm and ready to eat!

The properties of dough are very different from the properties of bread.

⦿ **Draw Conclusions** **Look** at the picture. **Write** how the dough changed.

_____

_____

_____

◁ Pipe cleaners can be bent into a new shape.

△ Paper can be folded into a new shape.

Mix and Separate Matter

You can stir matter together to make a mixture. A **mixture** is something made up of two or more kinds of matter. You can separate a mixture to see its parts.

Look at the fruit salad. It is a mixture of different kinds of fruit. You can separate the fruit in the salad. Each piece of fruit will stay the same.

Name another mixture.
Explain how you could separate it.

Separate this mixture into its parts.
Draw each part on its own plate.

Water Mixtures

Some mixtures are made with water. Look at the pictures. One mixture is made with sand and water. One mixture is made with salt and water. Sand and salt are solids.

You can separate these mixtures in different ways. You can let the solid matter sink. You can let the water evaporate. **Evaporate** means to change from a liquid to a gas.

Draw an X on the picture that shows a solid that sank.

Circle the picture that shows evaporation.

water with sand

water with salt

293

How can water change?

Envision It!

Tell how the ice is changing.

Inquiry Explore It!

How much water is in each cup?

Materials

crayon

3 plastic measuring cups (one with colored water)

☑ **1.** There are _____ **mL** in the first cup.

☑ **2.** Pour the liquid into another cup.
Measure. Record your data.

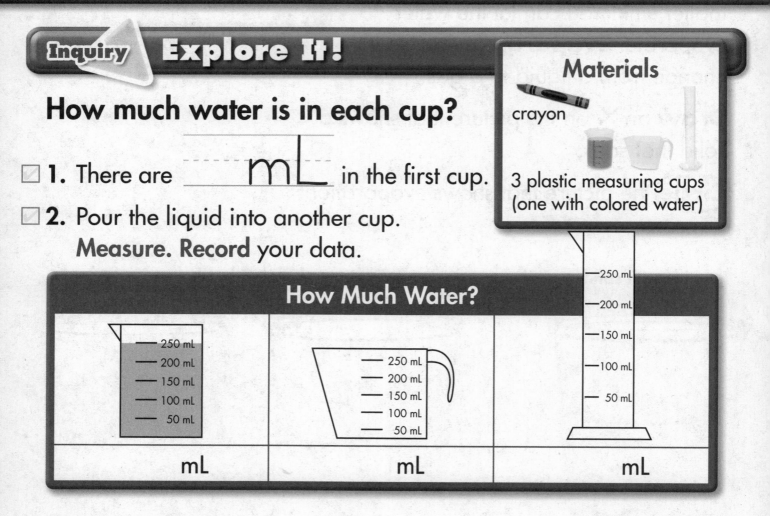

How Much Water?

— 250 mL — 200 mL — 150 mL — 100 mL — 50 mL	— 250 mL — 200 mL — 150 mL — 100 mL — 50 mL	—250 mL —200 mL —150 mL —100 mL — 50 mL
mL	mL	mL

Explain Your Results

3. Observe How did the volume and shape of the water change?

_____

_____

UNLOCK THE BIG ? I will know that water can be solid, liquid, or gas.

Word to Know

volume

Changing Shape

Matter can be changed. Water is matter. You can change the shape of water.

Suppose you pour a cup of water into a tall, thin container. The shape of the water will change. It looks like there is more liquid. However, the volume of the liquid is the same. **Volume** is the amount of space matter takes up. The volume of a liquid stays the same when it is poured into different kinds of containers.

Look at the pictures. **Tell** what shape the water takes.

The same amount of water was used to fill each of these containers.

295

Cooling Matter

Cooling can change the state of matter. Water can be a solid, a liquid, or a gas.

Water can change from a liquid to a solid. Suppose the air temperature is very cold. Rain will freeze and change to ice. Ice is a solid.

Water can change from a gas to a liquid too. Have you ever had a cold drink on a hot day? Water vapor in the air touches the cold glass. The water vapor changes from a gas to a liquid. Tiny drops of water form on the glass.

Water on these leaves changed from a liquid to a solid.

Lightning Lab

Effects of Temperature
Mix a teaspoon of sugar in a glass of cold water. Next, mix a teaspoon of sugar in a glass of very warm water. Tell how the temperature of the water affects what happens.

Look at the picture above. How is ice different from water?

_____

_____

_____

_____

_____

_____

_____

Heating Matter

Heating can change the state of matter too. Ice and snow melt when the air warms. Solid water becomes liquid.

Puddles evaporate into the air. The liquid water in the puddles changes to water vapor. Water vapor is a gas.

Suppose the temperature of water is very hot. Water boils and changes to water vapor. Water vapor is inside the bubbles of the boiling water.

Label the water as a solid, a liquid, or a gas. **Tell** about the water in each picture.

_____

_____

_____

Investigate It!

How can properties change?

Follow a Procedure

☐ **1.** Put 30 mL of glue in a measuring cup. **Observe** the properties of the glue. **Record.**

Substance Observations

Property	Glue	New Substance
Color		
Texture		
State of Matter (solid, liquid, gas)		

Materials

measuring cup

safety goggles

spoon

water

borax solution

glue and food coloring

Inquiry Skill

After making an observation you can **record** your data in a chart.

☐ **2.** Add two drops of food coloring.

Be careful! Wear safety goggles.

240CC

210CC

180CC

150CC

120CC

90CC

60CC

30CC

180CC

150CC

120CC

90CC

60CC

1cc = 1 mL

☐ **3.** Add 15 mL of water to the cup.
Stir the mixture. Observe its properties.

☐ **4.** Add 15 mL of borax solution.
Stir. Observe what happens.

☐ **5.** Observe the new substance.
Investigate its properties.
Record your observations.

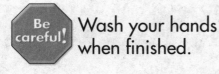
Be careful! Wash your hands when finished.

Analyze and Conclude

6. Compare the glue and the new substance.
How are the properties different?

_____

_____

_____

7. **Infer** Would the new substance
be a good glue? Explain.

_____

_____

_____

_____

From Sand to Glass

An artist made this glass sculpture. Glass is used in everyday objects such as eyeglasses too. Glass objects can look different. But they all have something in common. They are made from sand.

Glass is made mostly from melted sand. Sand melts at very high temperatures. The melted sand is soft. It hardens into glass when it cools.

Big World

My World

How is hot, melted sand different from glass?

_____

_____

_____

_____

_____

300

Vocabulary Smart Cards

matter
property
thermometer
solid
liquid
gas
physical
  change
mixture
evaporate
volume

Play a Game!

Cut out the cards.

Work with a partner.

Cover up the words.

Use the pictures to guess the words.

301

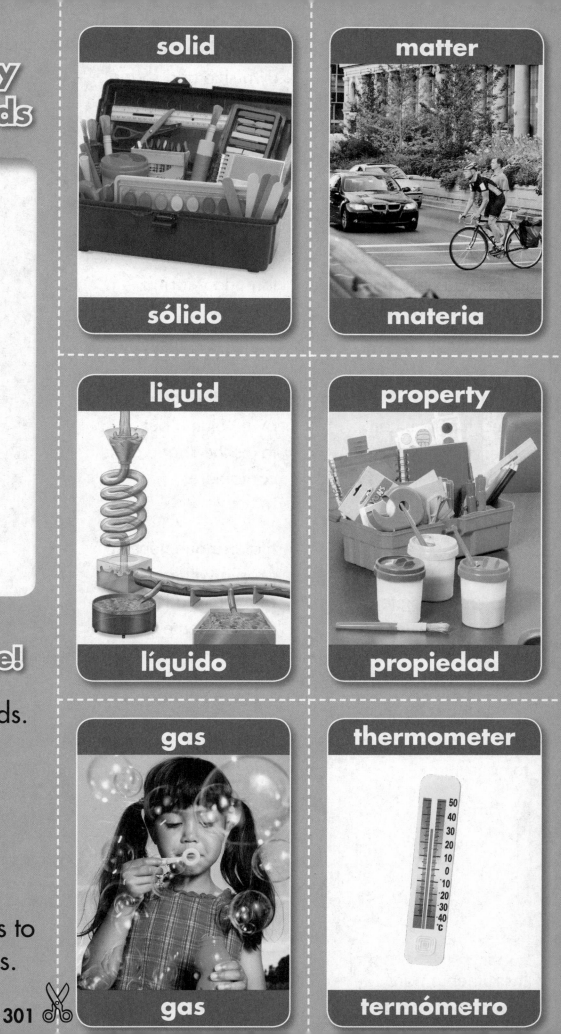

solid
sólido

matter
materia

liquid
líquido

property
propiedad

gas
gas

thermometer
termómetro

anything that takes up space and has mass

todo lo que ocupa espacio y tiene masa

matter that keeps its own size and shape

materia que mantiene tamaño y forma propios

something about an object that you can observe with your senses

algo en un objeto que puedes observar con tus sentidos

matter that has its own volume but takes the shape of its container

materia que tiene su propio volumen pero que toma la forma del recipiente que la contiene

a tool that measures temperature

instrumento para medir la temperatura

matter that does not have its own size or shape

materia que no tiene tamaño ni forma propios

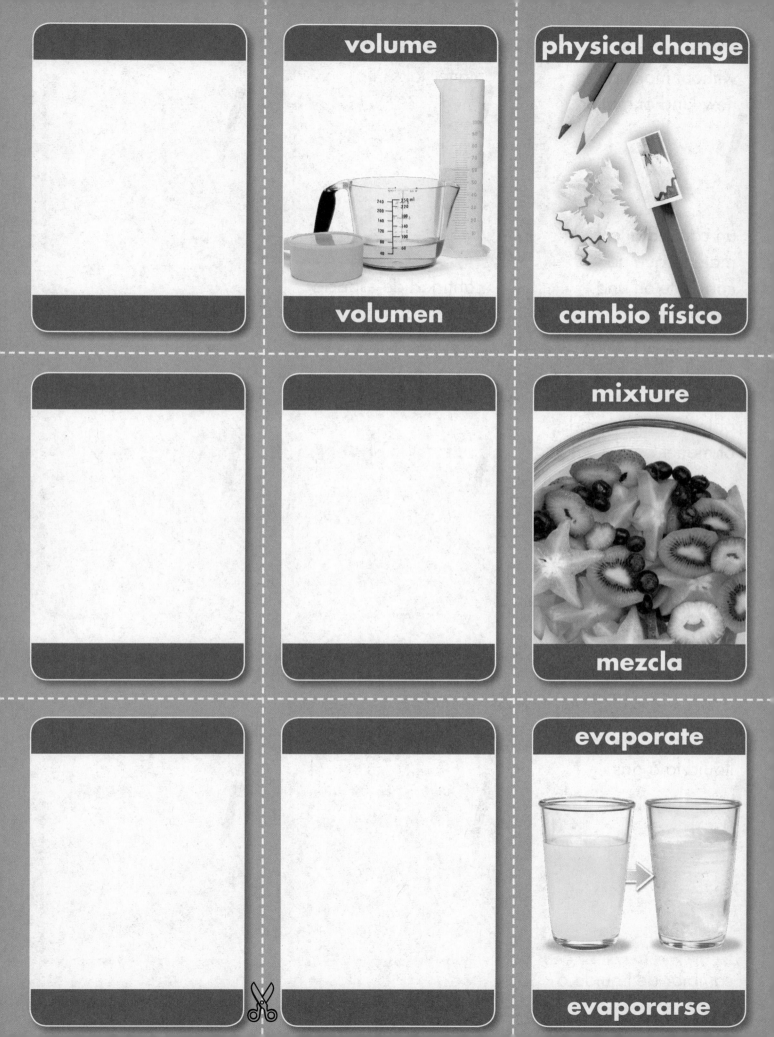

volume

volumen

physical change

cambio físico

mixture

mezcla

evaporate

evaporarse

a change to matter
without making it a
new kind of matter

un cambio a la
materia que no la
convierte en una
materia nueva

the amount of space
matter takes up

cantidad de espacio
que ocupa la materia

something made up
of two or more kinds
of matter

algo formado por
varios tipos de
materia

to change from a
liquid to a gas

cambiar de líquido a
gas

Study Guide

REVIEW THE BIG ? What is matter?

Physical Science

Lesson 1

What are some properties of matter?

- Temperature, weight, texture, and sinking or floating are properties of matter.

Lesson 2

What are solids, liquids, and gases?

- Solids keep their own shape. Liquids and gases take the shape of their containers.

Lesson 3

What are some ways matter can change?

- Cutting is a physical change.
- You can stir matter to make a mixture.

Lesson 4

How can water change?

- Water can be a solid, a liquid, or a gas.
- Volume is the amount of space matter takes up.

Chapter Review

REVIEW THE BIG ? **What is matter?**

Lesson 1

1. Vocabulary Write two things you know about matter.

_____

- -

_____

- -

_____

2. Evaluate (Circle) two objects that have a property that is the same. **Tell** about your answer.

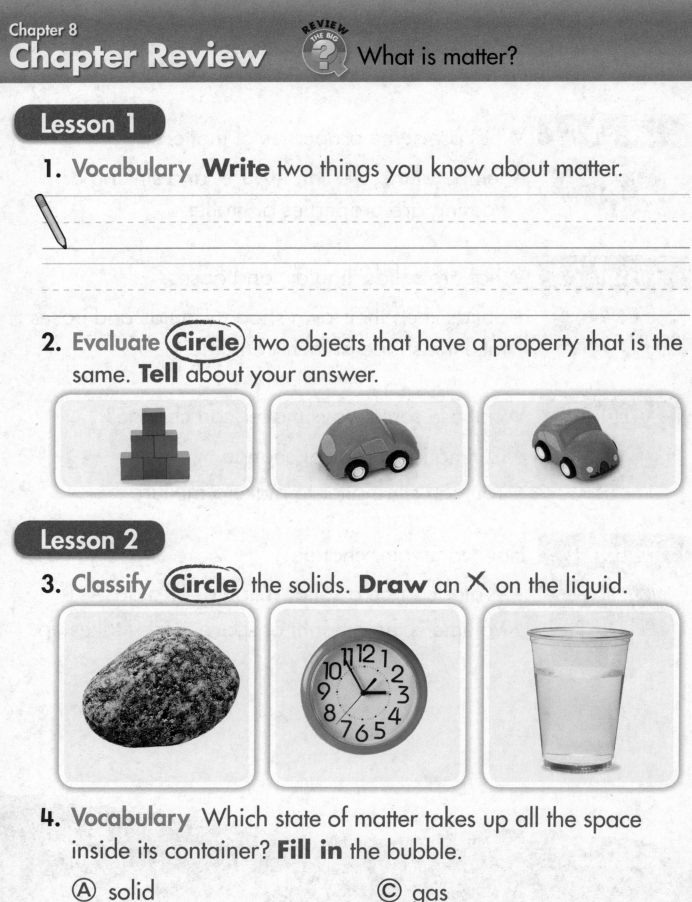

Lesson 2

3. Classify (Circle) the solids. **Draw** an X on the liquid.

4. Vocabulary Which state of matter takes up all the space inside its container? **Fill in** the bubble.

   Ⓐ solid   Ⓒ gas

   Ⓑ liquid   Ⓓ property

Lesson 3

◉ **5. Draw Conclusions Write** what made the candle melt.

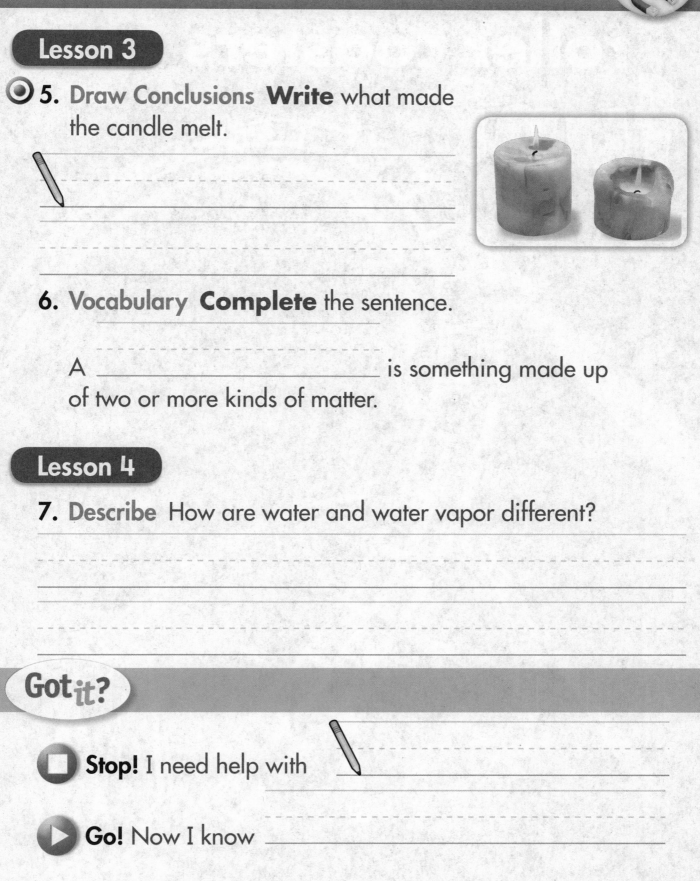

_____

_____

_____

_____

6. Vocabulary Complete the sentence.

_____

A _____ is something made up of two or more kinds of matter.

Lesson 4

7. Describe How are water and water vapor different?

_____

_____

_____

_____

_____

Got it?

☐ **Stop!** I need help with _____

_____

▶ **Go!** Now I know _____

What makes roller coasters
fun?

Energy, Motion, and Force

Chapter 9

Try It! How much force does it take to move objects?

Investigate It! How high will a ball bounce?

Trace the path of the roller coaster with your finger. **Tell** how the roller coaster moves.

THE BIG ? How do energy and forces make objects move?

Go to www.myscienceonline.com and click on: ⊗

Untamed Science
Sing and dance to an Ecogeek music video!

Got it? 60-Second Video
Lesson reviewed in a minute!

THE BIG ? I Will Know...
See what you've learned about science.

How much force does it take to move objects?

A force is a push or a pull. Force can be measured.

Be careful! Wear your safety goggles!

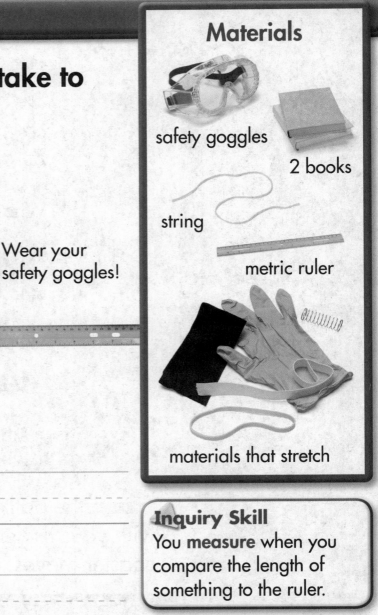

Materials

safety goggles

2 books

string

metric ruler

materials that stretch

□ **1.** Pick a material. Find a way to **measure** how much force it takes to move a book. **Record.**

□ **2.** Measure the force needed to move 2 books. Record.

Inquiry Skill
You **measure** when you compare the length of something to the ruler.

Explain Your Results

3. Explain how you **measured** force.

◉ **Cause and Effect**

A **cause** is what makes something happen. An **effect** is what happens.

Practice It!

This boy is playing baseball. The boy swings the bat. The boy hits the ball. The ball goes far. **Write** the effect of the boy hitting the ball.

Cause

The boy hits the ball.

➡

Effect

Lesson 1

What are some kinds of energy?

Envision It!

Circle the objects in this room that use electricity.

Inquiry **Explore It!**

What can light shine through?

Light is a form of energy.

☐ **1.** Shine the light at different objects and materials.

☐ **2.** Record what you observe.

Does light shine through?

	Clear Plastic (transparent)	Waxed Paper (translucent)	Black Paper (opaque)	Mirror (reflective)
Yes				
No				

Materials

flashlight

white paper

clear plastic

waxed paper

black paper

mirror

Be careful! Do not shine the light in anyone's eyes.

Explain Your Results

3. Communicate What objects can light shine through?

_____

_____

Words to Know

energy
electricity
reflect

Energy

People use energy in many ways. **Energy** is the ability to do work or cause change.

One kind of energy is **electricity.** Think about what happens when an air conditioner is turned on. The air conditioner uses electricity to cool your home. Electricity can warm your home too. A heater or a furnace can use electricity to warm your home.

This fan uses electricity to move air around your home.

Look at the fan in the picture. The fan uses electricity. **Tell** how you use electricity in your home.

313

Heat

Heat is the movement of energy from warmer places and objects to cooler ones.

People can use heat to cook their food. Look at the picture. Heat moves from the hot burner on the stove to the pot. Then heat moves from the hot pot to the cold food.

Draw arrows on the picture to show how heat is moving.

Heat from the stove cooks the food.

Light Energy

Light is another form of energy. Light comes from many sources. A lamp uses electricity to make light. A fire gives off light when it burns. Most light sources give off heat too.

The sun is our main source of light. Light travels from the sun to Earth. People, animals, and plants need the sun's light to live.

Underline the words that tell what light is.

Circle the sources of light in the picture.

315

How Light Moves

Light moves in straight lines. Different things can happen when light hits an object. Light can pass through some objects such as clear glass. Other objects let only some light pass through. Some objects block light. A shadow is made when something blocks light.

Tell two ways light can behave when it hits different objects.

◉ **Cause and Effect Look** at the picture. What causes the shadow of the table?

_____

_____

Light can move through clear glass. The glass is a transparent object.

The table blocks the light. The table is an opaque object.

The curtain lets only some light through. The curtain is a translucent material.

Light Reflects

Light can reflect off of an object. **Reflect** means to bounce off. Light reflects well from smooth, shiny objects such as mirrors. The picture shows how a mirror reflects light.

Cause and Effect What happens to light when it hits a mirror?

Draw an X under the spot on the mirror that reflects the light.

At-Home Lab

Mirrors and Light
Find a room with a mirror on the wall. Turn off all the lights. Shine a flashlight at the mirror. How does the direction of light change? Shine the light at a wall. Does the mirror reflect light better than the wall? Explain why.

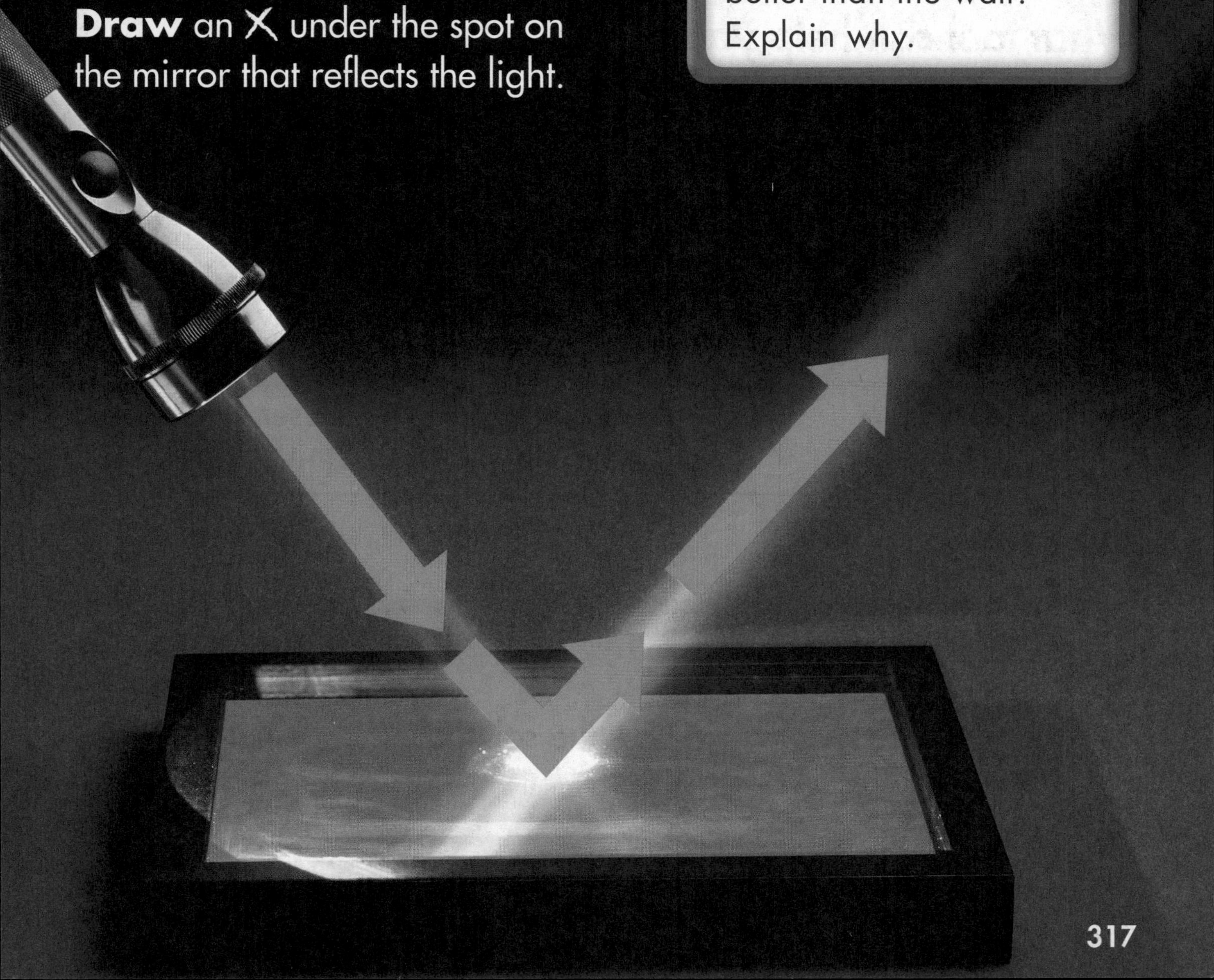

What is sound?

Envision It!

Draw one more instrument.

Inquiry Explore It!

What tool can help you see sound?

☑ 1. Look straight down at a vibration viewer. Use a deep voice. Softly say "Ahhhh" 3 cm from the cup. **Observe** the salt. **Record** what you see.

☑ 2. **Predict** what will happen if you say "Ahhhh" loudly. **Record.** Test your prediction.

Materials

safety goggles

vibration viewer

metric ruler

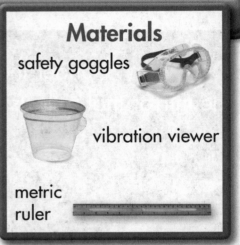

Observation "Ahhhh" Softly	Prediction "Ahhhh" Loudly	Observation "Ahhhh" Loudly

Explain Your Results

Be careful! Wear safety goggles.

3. **Communicate** Compare how the salt moved each time.

_____

_____

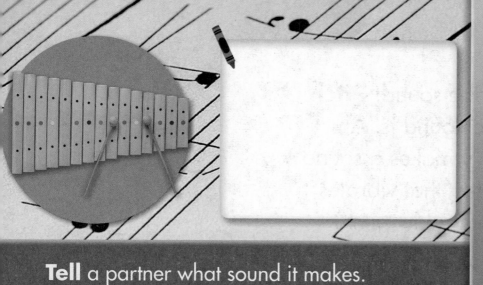

Tell a partner what sound it makes.

UNLOCK THE BIG ?

I will know what causes sound. I will know what pitch and volume are.

Words to Know

vibrate
pitch

Sound

The drummer hits the cymbal. You hear sound. Sound is a form of energy.

Sound is made when an object vibrates. **Vibrate** means to move quickly back and forth. A vibrating object makes the air around it vibrate. The vibrations travel through the air in waves. You hear the sound when the vibrations reach your ears.

⦿ Cause and Effect **Write** what causes a cymbal to make sound.

_____

_____

_____

The drum and cymbals make sounds when they vibrate.

319

Pitch

Pitch is one way to describe sound. **Pitch** means how high or low a sound is. An object that vibrates quickly makes a sound with a high pitch. An object that vibrates slowly makes a sound with a low pitch.

A guitar makes a sound when you pluck its strings. The pitch is high when the strings vibrate quickly. The pitch is low when the strings vibrate slowly.

Tell three objects that vibrate to make sound.

A tuba has a low pitch.

320

Look at the picture of the band.
Draw an ✗ on another instrument that you think has a high pitch.

Does the air blown into a tuba vibrate slowly or quickly? How do you know?

_____

_____

_____

Look at the ruler. It makes a sound when it vibrates.
Tell what pitch it has when it vibrates slowly.

A flute has a high pitch.
▽

Volume

Another way to describe sound is by its volume. Volume means how loud or soft a sound is.

Suppose you hit a drum very hard. The drum would vibrate strongly. The drum would make a loud sound. The sound would have a lot of energy.

Tell why you think the tool in the picture below makes a loud sound.

Draw something else that makes a loud sound.

LOUD

322

Suppose you lightly tap a drum. The drum would vibrate weakly. The drum would make a soft sound. The sound would not have much energy.

The picture on this page shows a soft sound. **Tell** how children can make a loud sound.

You hear an airplane while you are talking to your friend. **Tell** which sound has more energy. **Explain.**

SOFT

323

What are motion and force?

Draw an arrow to show which way the rope is moving.

my planet Diary ← Connections →

Read Together

The ancient Egyptians built these pyramids a long time ago. The ancient Egyptians lived before trucks and cranes. It was hard to move the heavy stones they needed.

The ancient Egyptians were good problem solvers. They may have pushed the heavy stones up dirt ramps. They moved the stones all the way to the top of the pyramids!

How might the pyramids be built today?

_____

_____

_____

Words to Know

motion
force

Motion

Motion is the act of moving. Objects can move in different ways.

A swing can move back and forth. The blades of a fan move round and round. You push a toy truck across the floor. The truck moves in a straight line. You may move the truck in a curve or a zigzag motion too. Zigzag means you push the truck one way and then another way.

Tell how the merry-go-round moves.

○ Cause and Effect **Write** the effect of pushing the toy truck.

Cause	Effect
You push the truck across the floor.	

Force

You can move things in different ways. A push or a pull that makes something move is called a **force.** A force changes the way an object moves.

You need to apply more force to move heavier objects than lighter ones. Suppose you are pushing a shopping cart. The cart is easier to move when it is empty. The cart is harder to move when it is full.

Would you need more force to move a book or a pencil? **Tell** how you know.

Lightning Lab

Forces and Movement
Get a ball. Use a force. Push or pull the ball. Show how you can change the way the ball moves. Try a different object. Compare the different ways the objects moved.

Look at the boy on the slide.
Draw an arrow to show how he will move.

A push helps the girls go up and down on the seesaw.

Direction

An object will move in the direction it is pushed or pulled. Suppose you change the direction of the force. The object will move in a different direction.

Objects can move toward or away from something. Someone kicks you a ball. The ball moves toward you. You kick it back. The ball moves away from you.

Objects can move up and down. You push up a window to open it. You pull down a window to close it.

Look at the pictures.
Complete the sentences.

The girl kicks the ball

_____

- - - - - - - - - - - -

_____

from her.

Fast and Slow, Near and Far

The speed of an object depends on the amount of force that is used to move it. Speed is how fast or slow an object moves.

How far an object moves depends on how much force is used. It takes more force to move objects farther.

How fast and far an object moves depends on the surface. A ball can move fast and far on a hard, smooth surface. It will not move as fast or far on a rough or soft surface.

Cause and Effect You push a wooden block across the floor. **Tell** what can change how fast and far the block moves.

The boy kicks the ball hard. It will move _____ .

329

What are magnets?

Why do the letters stay on the refrigerator?

Inquiry Explore It!

What can a magnet pull through?

☐ **1.** Put a paper clip in a cup.
Hold the magnet as shown.

☐ **2. Record** what you **observe.**

Materials

magnet

paper square

paper clip

plastic cup with water

plastic cup

Can a magnet pull through these things?

	Plastic	Water	Air	Paper
	solid	liquid	gas	solid
Yes				
No				

Explain Your Results

3. Interpret Data What can the magnet pull through?

_____

- -

_____

tnae

They are __ __ __ __ __ __ __.

UNLOCK THE BIG ?

I will know that magnets can push or pull some metal objects.

Words to Know

attract

repel

Magnets

Magnets can push or pull some metal objects.

Magnets attract some metal objects. **Attract** means to pull toward.

Magnets can repel other magnets. **Repel** means to push away.

The ability to attract and repel objects is a property of matter.

● **Cause and Effect** (Circle) the objects that are attracted to the magnet. **Draw** an X on the objects that are not attracted.

Tell why some of the objects were not attracted to the magnet.

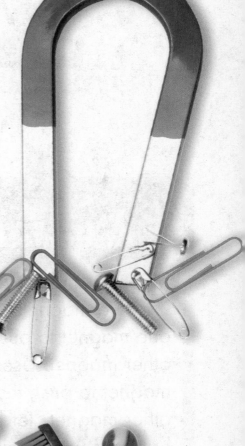

331

Magnet Poles

Magnets have poles. A pole is the place on a magnet that has the strongest push or pull. Look at the poles of the magnets. The N stands for north pole. The S stands for south pole.

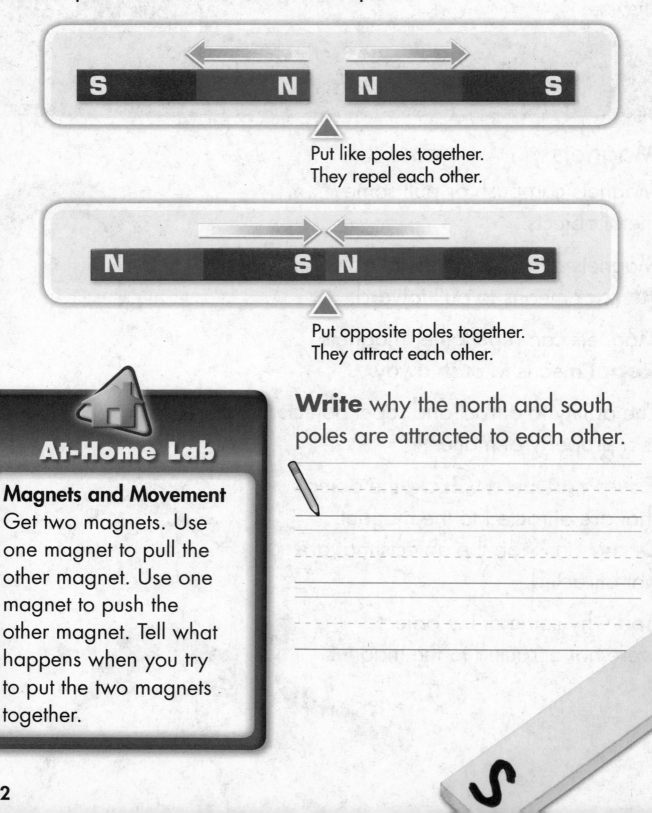

Put like poles together. They repel each other.

Put opposite poles together. They attract each other.

At-Home Lab

Magnets and Movement
Get two magnets. Use one magnet to pull the other magnet. Use one magnet to push the other magnet. Tell what happens when you try to put the two magnets together.

Write why the north and south poles are attracted to each other.

How Magnets Move Objects

A magnet can move some things without touching them. Look at the picture below. The spoon is moving toward the magnet. The magnet is not touching the spoon. The force of the magnet pulls the spoon.

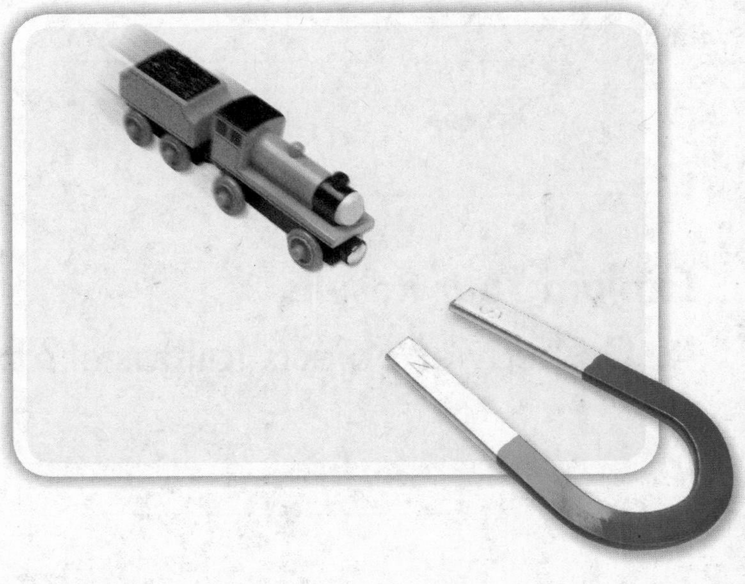

◎ **Cause and Effect**
Draw an arrow to show which way the train will move.

What is gravity?

Draw a line to show how the basketball will move.

Inquiry Explore It!

How do heavier objects fall?

☐ **1.** Put five marbles in one bag. Put ten in another. Seal the bags.

☐ **2.** Hold both bags at the same height. Drop them at the same time. Repeat three times.

☐ **3.** **Record** your **observations.**

_____

_____

_____

Materials

15 metal marbles

2 resealable plastic bags

Explain Your Results

4. Do heavier objects fall faster? Explain using your **observations.**

_____

_____

_____

UNLOCK THE BIG ? I will know that gravity pulls things toward the center of Earth.

Word to Know

gravity

Gravity

Gravity is a pulling force. Gravity pulls things toward the center of Earth. Look at the girl jumping in the air. She will not float up. Gravity will pull her down.

Think about when it rains. Gravity is the force that pulls the rain down to the ground.

◎ **Cause and Effect** **Write** what would happen if gravity did not pull on the leaves in the picture.

_____

_____

_____

_____

_____

335

Gravity and Weight

Look at the girl playing with the toy. Gravity is pulling the toy down. Gravity pulls things toward the ground unless something holds them up.

How much something weighs tells how strong the pull of gravity is on it. The table weighs more than the toy drum. The pull of gravity is stronger on the table than on the toy drum.

Draw an arrow to show how the toy moves because of gravity.

Write why the toy bear does not fall to the ground.

_____

_____

_____

_____

_____

Write whether the pull of gravity is stronger on the girl or on the balls. **Tell** how you know.

_____

_____

_____

_____

Lightning Lab

Sink or Float
Make a boat using foil. Put the boat in a bowl of water. Add pennies one at a time. Tell how many pennies you added before the boat sank.

How high will a ball bounce?

Follow a Procedure

☐ **1.** Tape a meterstick to a wall.

Drop the ball from 50 cm.

Measure how high it bounces.

Record.

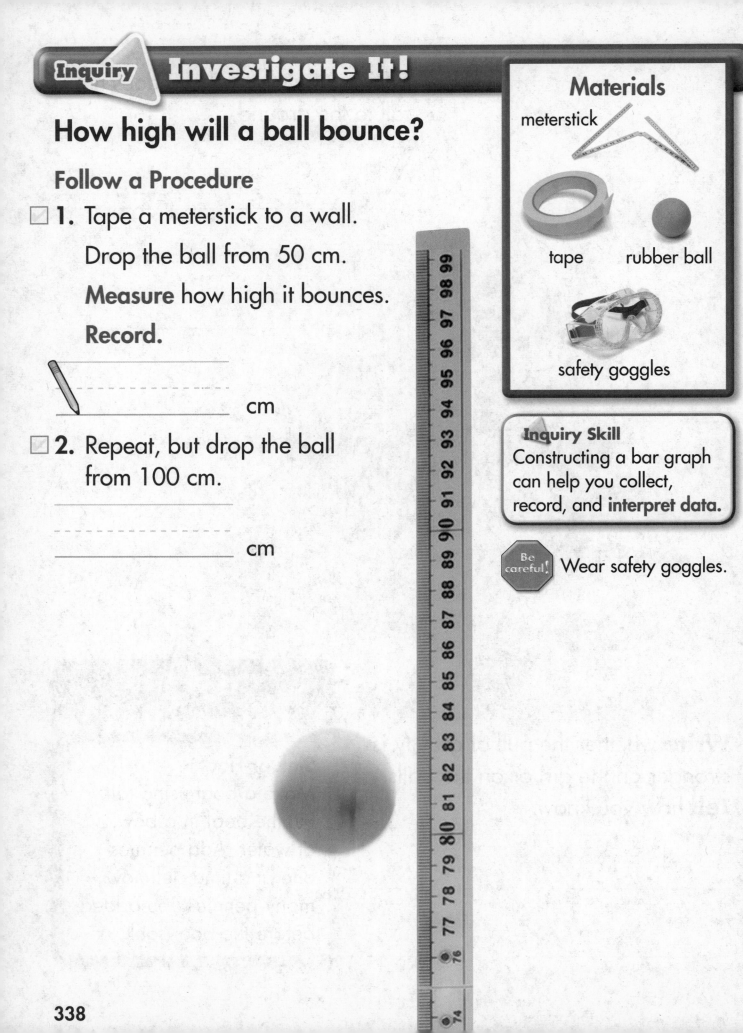

_____ cm

☐ **2.** Repeat, but drop the ball from 100 cm.

_____ cm

Materials

meterstick

tape   rubber ball

safety goggles

Inquiry Skill
Constructing a bar graph can help you collect, record, and **interpret data.**

Be careful! Wear safety goggles.

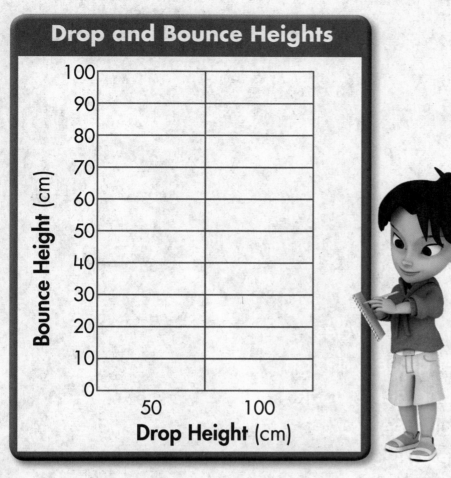

Drop and Bounce Heights

Bounce Height (cm): 0, 10, 20, 30, 40, 50, 60, 70, 80, 90, 100

Drop Height (cm): 50, 100

Analyze and Conclude

3. Interpret Data   When did the ball bounce higher?

_____

_____

4. Infer   What force pulled the ball to the ground?

_____

_____

5. UNLOCK THE BIG ?   How did the height you dropped the ball from affect how high the ball bounced?

_____

_____

_____

Bicycles

Engineers design machines. Bicycles are machines. Bicycle engineers design and improve bicycles. Engineers added pedals to bicycles. Pedals need force to move. Riders push pedals to move the bicycle. Some engineers work on parts of a bicycle that make you safe. One part that keeps you safe is a rear light. Rear lights make bicycles easier to see. Engineers also make bicycles that can last a long time. Engineers change materials and improve the technology used to build better bicycles.

Other than rear lights, how do you think engineers have improved bicycles?

Vocabulary Smart Cards

energy
electricity
reflect
vibrate
pitch
motion
force
attract
repel
gravity

Play a Game!

Cut out the cards.

Work with a partner.

Pick a card.

Say clues about the word.

Have your partner guess the word.

341

vibrate
vibrar

pitch
tono

motion
movimiento

energy
energía

electricity
electricidad

reflect
reflejar

the ability to do work
or cause change

capacidad de hacer
trabajo o causar
cambio

to move quickly back
and forth

moverse rápidamente
hacia delante y hacia
atrás

a kind of energy that
can flow through
wires and make light
and heat

tipo de energía que
puede fluir por cables
y generar luz y calor

how high or low a
sound is

cuán agudo o grave
es un sonido

to bounce off

rebotar

the act of moving

el acto de moverse

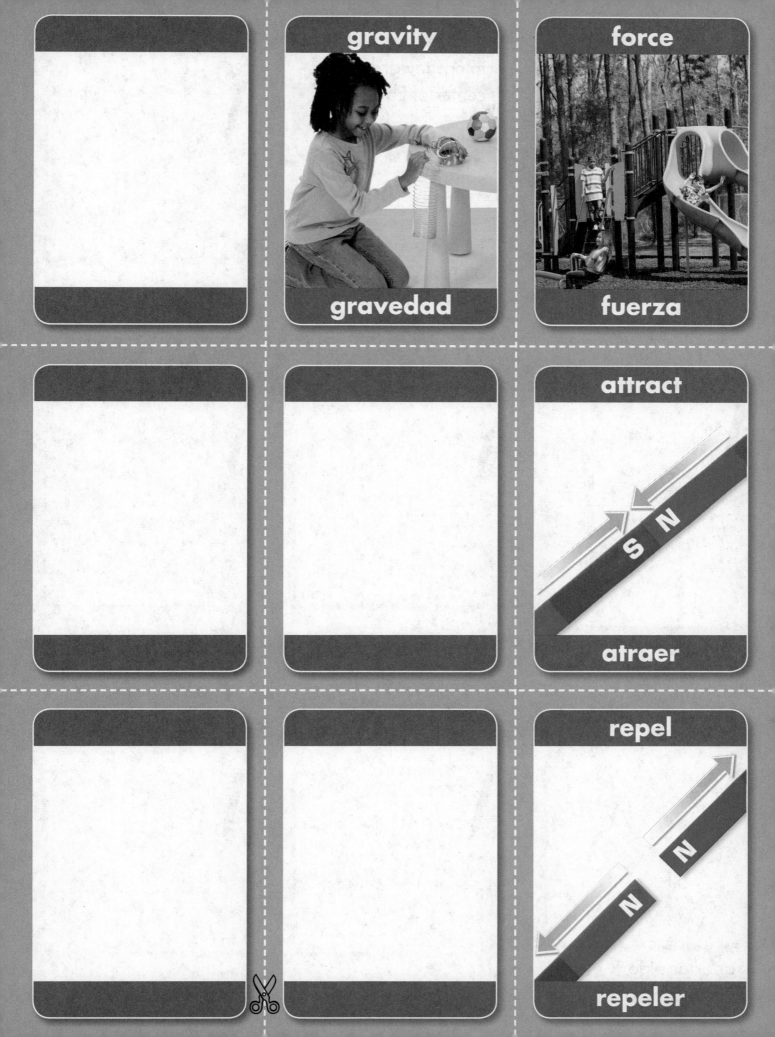

gravity

gravedad

force

fuerza

attract

atraer

repel

repeler

a push or pull that makes something move

empujón o jalón que hace que algo se mueva

a force that pulls things toward the center of Earth

fuerza que jala los objetos hacia el centro de la Tierra

to pull toward

jalar hacia sí

to push away

apartar algo empujándolo

REVIEW THE BIG ? How do energy and forces make objects move?

Lesson 1

What are some kinds of energy?

- Electricity and light are kinds of energy.
- Light reflects from smooth, shiny objects.

Lesson 2

What is sound?

- Objects vibrate to make sound.
- Pitch and volume are ways to describe sound.

Lesson 3

What are motion and force?

- Motion is the act of moving.
- Force is a push or pull that makes objects move.

Lesson 4

What are magnets?

- Magnets attract some objects and repel other objects.

Lesson 5

What is gravity?

- Gravity is a force that pulls objects toward the ground unless something holds them up.

Lesson 1

1. **Infer** (Circle) the object that uses electricity. **Write** how you know.

_____

2. **Compare** Which object reflects light best? **Fill in** the bubble.

   Ⓐ shadow   Ⓒ rough wall
   Ⓑ clear glass   Ⓓ mirror

Lesson 2

3. **Describe** **Name** two objects that vibrate to make sound.

_____

_____

4. **Vocabulary** **Draw** an ✗ on the instrument that has a higher pitch.

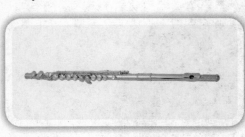 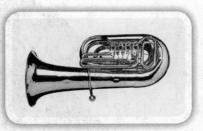

Lesson 3

5. Apply Draw lines to show two ways the car can move.

Lesson 4

6. Vocabulary Complete the sentence.

Like poles on magnets _____ each other.

Lesson 5

7. Cause and Effect Write what force causes objects to fall to the ground.

_____

_____

_____

Got it?

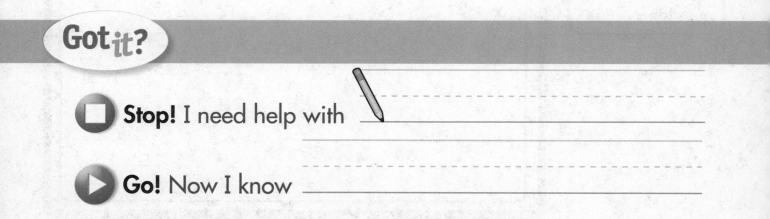

Stop! I need help with _____

_____

_____

Go! Now I know _____

ow does a seesaw work?

Materials

toy car

eraser

pennies

ruler with plastic cups (prepared by teacher)

Ask a question.

How can a smaller person lift a bigger person on a seesaw? Use a ruler to find out.

Make a prediction.

1. If you move one cup closer to the middle of a ruler, will you need more or fewer pennies to lift the other cup?

(a) more pennies

(b) fewer pennies

Plan a fair test.

Use two cups that are the same size.

Inquiry Skill
You plan an **experiment** when you design a way to answer a scientific question.

Design your test.

☑ **2.** Make a seesaw model. Draw it in the chart.

☑ **3.** List your steps.

Do your test.

☑ **4.** Follow your steps.

Collect and record data.

☐ **5.** Fill in the chart.

Tell your conclusion.

6. When did you use fewer pennies?

_____

_____

7. Communicate How can a smaller person lift a bigger person on a seesaw?

_____

_____

_____

_____

Performance-Based Assessment

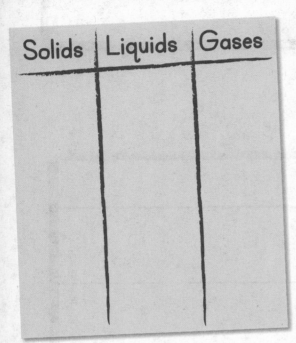

Solids	Liquids	Gases

Make a Chart

- Make a chart with three columns.
- Label the columns Solids, Liquids, and Gases.
- Write words or draw pictures in the columns to show solids, liquids, and gases.

Write a Fable

- A fable is a story that is made up to teach a lesson.
- Write a fable that teaches a lesson about why everything that goes up must come down.

Using Scientific Methods

1. Ask a question.
2. Make a hypothesis.
3. Plan a fair test.
4. Do your test.
5. Collect and record data.
6. Draw a conclusion.

Changing Speed and Position

- Find toy cars with wheels of different sizes.
- Investigate how wheel size affects how fast the toy cars can go.
- Show other ways the cars can move.

Measurements

Metric and Customary Measurements

Science uses the metric system to measure things.
Metric measurement is used around the world.
Here is how different metric measurements
compare to customary measurements.

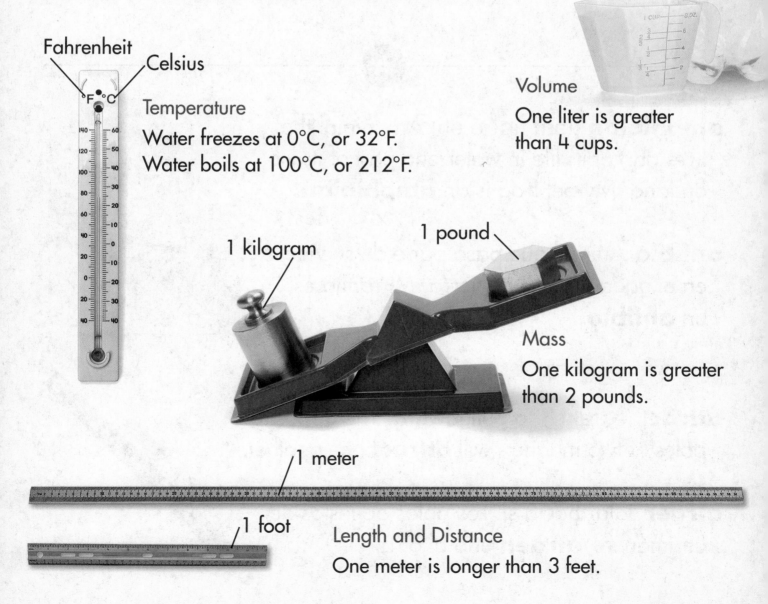

1 liter

1 cup

Volume
One liter is greater
than 4 cups.

Fahrenheit
Celsius

Temperature
Water freezes at 0°C, or 32°F.
Water boils at 100°C, or 212°F.

1 kilogram

1 pound

Mass
One kilogram is greater
than 2 pounds.

1 meter

1 foot

Length and Distance
One meter is longer than 3 feet.

Glossary

The glossary uses letters and signs to show how words are pronounced. The mark ′ is placed after a syllable with a primary or heavy accent. The mark ′ is placed after a syllable with a secondary or lighter accent.

To hear these vocabulary words and definitions, you can refer to the AudioText CD, or log on to the digital path's Vocabulary Smart Cards.

Pronunciation Key

a	in hat	ō	in open	sh	in she
ā	in age	ȯ	in all	th	in thin
â	in care	ô	in order	ŦH	in then
ä	in far	oi	in oil	zh	in measure
e	in let	ou	in out	ə	= a in about
ē	in equal	u	in cup	ə	= e in taken
ėr	in term	u̇	in put	ə	= i in pencil
i	in it	ü	in rule	ə	= o in lemon
ī	in ice	ch	in child	ə	= u in circus
o	in hot	ng	in long		

A

amphibian (am fib′ ē ən) An animal that lives part of its life in water and part of its life on land. My pet frog is an **amphibian.**

anfibio Animal que pasa parte de su vida en el agua y parte en tierra. Mi ranita es un **anfibio.**

attract (ə trakt′) To pull toward. The opposite poles of two magnets will **attract** one another.

atraer Jalar hacia sí. Los polos opuestos de un imán **se atraen** uno al otro.

C

camouflage (kam′ ə fläzh) A color or shape that makes an animal hard to see. Some animals use **camouflage** to hide themselves.

camuflaje Color o forma que hace que un animal sea difícil de ver. Algunos animales usan **camuflaje** para esconderse.

conclusion (kən klü′ zhən) What you decide after you think about all you know. Scientists repeat their tests before drawing a **conclusion.**

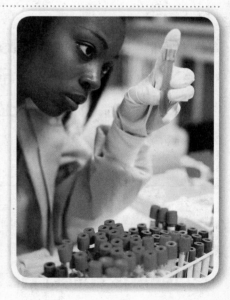

conclusión Lo que decides después de pensar en lo que sabes. Los científicos repiten sus pruebas antes de sacar una **conclusión.**

constellation (kon′ stə lā′ shən) A group of stars that forms a picture. I like to search the night sky for **constellations.**

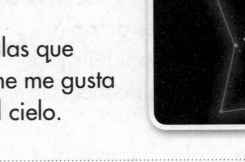

constelación Grupo de estrellas que forman una figura. Por la noche me gusta buscar **constelaciones** en el cielo.

crater (krā′ tər) A hole in the ground shaped like a bowl. There are many **craters** on the surface of the moon.

cráter Hueco con forma de tazón que se encuentra en la tierra. Hay muchos **cráteres** en la superficie de la Luna.

D

data (dā′ tə) What you observe. Scientists collect **data** while working.

datos Lo que observas. Los científicos reúnen **datos** cuando trabajan.

electricity (i lek′ tris′ ə tē) A kind of energy that can flow through wires and make light and heat. A computer uses **electricity** to work.

electricidad Tipo de energía que puede fluir por cables y generar luz y calor. Una computadora funciona con **electricidad.**

energy (en′ ər jē) The ability to do work or cause change. A fan uses **energy** to move air around a home.

energía Capacidad de hacer trabajo o causar cambio. Un abanico usa **energía** para mover el aire dentro de una casa.

evaporate (i vap′ ə rāt) To change from a liquid to a gas. Water **evaporates** when it changes into water vapor.

evaporarse Cambiar de líquido a gas. El agua se **evapora** cuando se convierte en vapor de agua.

extinct (ek stingkt′) A plant or animal that no longer lives on Earth. Dinosaurs are **extinct.**

extinto Planta o animal que ya no existe en la Tierra. Los dinosaurios están **extintos.**

F

food chain (füd chān) A model that shows how energy passes from one living thing to another. Plants are part of **food chains.**

cadena alimentaria Modelo que muestra cómo se transmite la energía de un ser vivo a otro. Las plantas forman parte de **cadenas alimentarias.**

force (fôrs) A push or pull that makes something move. A **force** helps children go down the slide.

fuerza Empujón o jalón que hace que algo se mueva. Una **fuerza** ayuda a los niños a bajar por el tobogán.

fossil (fos′ əl) A print or part of a plant or animal that lived long ago. The scientist found a dragonfly **fossil.**

fósil Huella o parte de una planta o animal que vivió hace mucho tiempo. El científico encontró el **fósil** de una libélula.

fuel (fyü′ əl) Anything that is used to make heat or power. Wood can be used as **fuel** for a campfire.

combustible Cualquier cosa que se usa para generar calor o energía. La madera se puede usar como **combustible** para una fogata.

G

gas (gas) Matter that does not have its own size or shape. Bubbles are filled with **gas.**

gas Materia que no tiene tamaño ni forma propios. Las burbujas están llenas de **gas.**

glacier (glā′ shər) A large body of moving ice. **Glaciers** can be found in the Arctic.

glaciar Gran masa de hielo que se mueve. En el Ártico hay **glaciares.**

goal (gōl) Something you want to do. People set a **goal** to find a solution.

objetivo Algo que quieres hacer. Escogemos un **objetivo** para encontrar una solución.

gravity (grav′ ə tē) A force that pulls things toward the center of Earth. **Gravity** is pulling the toy down.

gravedad Fuerza que jala los objetos hacia el centro de la Tierra. La **gravedad** jala el juguete hacia abajo.

H

habitat (hab′ ə tat) A place where a plant or animal lives. An arctic fox lives in a cold **habitat.**

hábitat Un lugar donde vive una planta o un animal. Un zorro ártico vive en un **hábitat** frío.

hypothesis (hī poth′ ə sis) A possible answer to a question. Scientists decide if a **hypothesis** is supported or not supported.

hipótesis Respuesta posible a una pregunta. Los científicos deciden si una **hipótesis** tiene bases firmes o no.

inherit (in her′ it) To get from a parent. Children **inherit** hair color.

heredar Recibir de un progenitor. Los niños **heredan** el color de pelo.

inquiry (in kwī′ rē) Asking questions and looking for answers. Scientists use **inquiry** to learn.

indagación Hacer preguntas y buscar respuestas. Los científicos hacen **indagaciones** para aprender.

invent (in vent′) To make something for the first time. Scientists **invented** cars that use both gasoline and electricity.

inventar Hacer algo por primera vez. Los científicos **inventaron** carros que usan tanto gasolina como electricidad.

landform (land′ fôrm) A natural feature on Earth. A plain is one kind of **landform.**

accidente geográfico Formación natural en la Tierra. Una llanura es un tipo de **accidente geográfico.**

larva (lär′ və) A young insect. A butterfly **larva** is called a caterpillar.

larva Una insecto joven. La **larva** de una mariposa se llama oruga.

life cycle (līf sī′ kəl) The way a living thing grows and changes. We studied the **life cycle** of a butterfly.

ciclo de vida Manera en que un ser vivo crece y cambia. Hoy estudiamos el **ciclo de vida** de la mariposa.

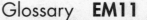

liquid (lik′ wid) Matter that has its own volume but takes the shape of its container. The **liquid** changes shape in the tubes.

líquido Materia que tiene su propio volumen pero que toma la forma del recipiente que la contiene. El **líquido** cambia de forma dentro de los tubos.

litter (lit′ ər) All the babies born to a mammal at the same time. There is a **litter** of mice in the nest.

camada Todos los bebés nacidos de un mamífero al mismo tiempo. Hay una **camada** de ratones en el nido.

loam (lōm) Soil that is made of sand, silt, clay, and pieces of living things that have died. Most plants grow best in **loam.**

marga Suelo formado por arena, cieno, arcilla y pedazos de cosas vivas que han muerto. La mayoría de las plantas crecen mejor en la **marga.**

material (mə tir′ ē əl) What something is made of. Fleece is a soft **material.**

material De lo que está hecho algo. El tejido polar es un **material** suave.

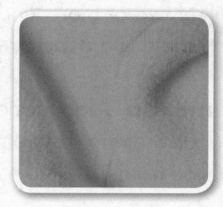

matter (mat′ ər) Anything that takes up space and has mass. Everything is made of **matter.**

materia Todo lo que ocupa espacio y tiene masa. Todo está hecho de **materia.**

mineral (min′ ə rəl) A nonliving material that comes from Earth. Quartz is a **mineral.**

mineral Un material sin vida que viene de la Tierra. El cuarzo es un **mineral.**

mixture (miks′ chər) Something made up of two or more kinds of matter. This fruit salad is a **mixture** of different fruits.

mezcla Algo formado por varios tipos de materia. Esta ensalada es una **mezcla** de frutas.

motion (mō′ shən) The act of moving. A merry-go-round moves in a circular **motion.**

movimiento El acto de moverse. Los carruseles siguen un **movimiento** circular.

N

natural resource (nach′ ər əl rē′ sôrs) A useful material that comes from Earth. Water is a **natural resource.**

recurso natural Un material útil que proviene de la Tierra. El agua es un **recurso natural.**

nutrient (nü′ trē ənt) A material that living things need to live and grow. Many plants get **nutrients** from soil and water.

nutriente Un material que los seres vivos necesitan para vivir y crecer. Muchas plantas obtienen **nutrientes** del suelo y del agua.

observe (əb sėrv′) To use your senses to find out about something. You can **observe** how an apple looks, sounds, feels, smells, and tastes.

observar Usar tus sentidos para descubrir algo. Puedes **observar** el aspecto de una manzana, cómo suena, cómo es cuando la tocas, a qué huele y a qué sabe.

pattern (pat′ ərn) The way something repeats itself. Weather follows a **pattern.**

patrón La manera en que algo se repite. El tiempo sigue un **patrón.**

phase (fāz) The shape of the lighted part of the moon. The moon's **phases** can be seen best at night.

fase Forma de la parte iluminada de la Luna. Las **fases** de la Luna se ven mejor de noche.

physical change (fiz′ ə kəl chānj) A change to matter without making it a new kind of matter. Sharpening a pencil causes a **physical change.**

cambio físico Un cambio a la materia que no la convierte en una materia nueva. Afilar la punta de un lápiz causa un **cambio físico.**

pitch (pich) How high or low a sound is. The musical note had a very high **pitch.**

tono Cuán agudo o grave es un sonido. La nota musical tenía un **tono** muy alto.

pollution (pə lü′ shən) Something harmful added to land, air, or water. Many people work hard to reduce **pollution.**

contaminación Algo dañino que se desecha en la tierra, el aire o el agua. Mucha gente se esfuerza por reducir la **contaminación.**

precipitation (pri sip′ ə tā′ shən) The water that falls to Earth. Rain is a kind of **precipitation.**

precipitación El agua que cae a la Tierra. La lluvia es una forma de **precipitación.**

predator (pred′ ə tər) An animal that catches and eats another animal. A hawk is a fierce **predator.**

predador Animal que caza y se alimenta de otro animal. El halcón es un **predador** feroz.

prey (prā) An animal that is caught and eaten. Voles are **prey.**

presa Animal que es cazado y comido. Las ratas de campo sirven de **presa.**

property (prop′ ər tē) Something about an object that you can observe with your senses. An object's color is one kind of **property.**

propiedad Algo en un objeto que puedes observar con tus sentidos. El color de un objeto es una **propiedad** de ese objeto.

pupa (pyü′ pə) Stage in an insect's life between larva and adult. When a caterpillar is changing inside its covering, it is called a **pupa.**

pupa Etapa de la vida de un insecto entre larva y adulto. Cuando la oruga cambia dentro de la cubierta que la protege, se llama **pupa.**

R

recycle (rē sī′ kəl) To change something so it can be used again. My family **recycles** plastic milk containers.

reciclar Cambiar algo de manera que se pueda usar otra vez. Mi familia **recicla** envases plásticos para leche.

reflect (ri flekt′) To bounce off. Light can **reflect** off a mirror.

reflejar Rebotar. La luz puede **reflejarse** en un espejo.

refuge (ref′ yüj) A safe place to live. You can see plants and animals at a **refuge.**

refugio Lugar seguro para vivir. Puedes ver plantas y animales en un **refugio.**

repel (ri pel′) To push away. The north ends of magnets will **repel** each other.

repeler Apartar algo empujándolo. Los polos norte de dos imanes se **repelen** uno al otro.

rock (rok) A hard, solid part of Earth that is not soil or metal. José collects **rocks.**

roca Una parte dura y sólida de la Tierra que no es suelo o metal. José colecciona **rocas.**

roots (rütz) Parts of the plant that hold the plant in place and take in water and nutrients. **Roots** grow into the soil.

raíces Partes de la planta que la matienen en su lugar y que absorben agua y nutrientes. Las **raíces** al crecer se entierran en el suelo.

S

seedling (sēd′ ling) A young plant. The tree **seedling** grows into a tree.

plántula Una planta joven. La **plántula** crece y se convierte en un árbol.

severe weather (sə vir′ weŦH′ ər) Dangerous weather. It is important to be ready for **severe weather.**

tiempo severo Tiempo peligroso. Es importante estar preparado para el **tiempo severo.**

simple machine (sim′ pəl mə shēn′) Tool with few or no moving parts. A **simple machine** can make work easier.

máquina simple Instrumento sin, o con pocas, partes que se mueven. Una **máquina simple** puede hacer que el trabajo sea más fácil.

skeleton (skel′ ə tən) All the bones of the body fitted together. Your **skeleton** protects the inside parts of your body.

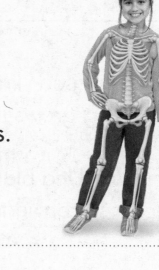

esqueleto Todos los huesos del cuerpo juntos. El **esqueleto** protege las partes internas del cuerpo.

soil (soil) The top layer of Earth. **Soil** helps plants grow.

suelo La capa superior de la Tierra. El **suelo** ayuda a que las plantas crezcan.

solar system (sō′ lər sis′ təm) The sun, the planets and their moons, and other objects that move around the sun. Earth is part of the **solar system.**

sistema solar El Sol, los planetas con sus satélites y otros objetos que giran alrededor del Sol. La Tierra es parte del **sistema solar.**

solid (sol′ id) Matter that keeps its own size and shape. The case that holds the supplies is a **solid.**

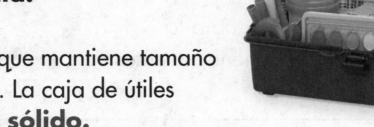

sólido Materia que mantiene tamaño y forma propios. La caja de útiles de pintura es un **sólido.**

star (stär) A ball of burning gases that gives off light and heat. There are many **stars** in the night sky.

estrella Bola de gases muy calientes que produce calor y luz. De noche hay muchas **estrellas** en el cielo.

stem (stem) Part of the plant that carries water and nutrients to the leaves. Some plants have a straight **stem.**

tallo Parte de la planta que lleva el agua y los nutrientes a las hojas. Algunas plantas tienen el **tallo** derecho.

sun (sun) The closest star to Earth. The **sun** keeps us warm.

Sol La estrella más cercana a la Tierra. El **Sol** nos mantiene calientes.

T

tadpole (tad′ pōl) A very young frog. Rosie caught **tadpoles** in a pond.

renacuajo Una rana muy joven. Rosie atrapó **renacuajos** en el estanque.

technology (tek nol′ ə jē) The use of science to solve problems. People use **technology** every day.

tecnología El uso de la ciencia para resolver problemas. Usamos la **tecnología** todos los días.

temperature (tem′ pər ə chər) How hot or cold something is. The **temperature** is higher in the summer, when it is warmer.

26° C
(79° F)

temperatura Cuán caliente o fría está una cosa. La **temperatura** es más alta en verano, cuando hace calor.

texture (teks′ chər) How something feels. Clay soil has a sticky **texture.**

textura Cómo se siente algo al tacto. La arcilla tiene una **textura** pegajosa.

thermometer (thər mom′ ə tər) A tool that measures temperature. You can use a **thermometer** to measure how hot or cold something is.

termómetro Instrumento para medir la temperatura. Puedes usar un **termómetro** para medir cuán caliente o cuán frío está algo.

tool (tül) Something that is used to do work. Some **tools** are used to observe.

instrumento Algo que se usa para hacer trabajo. Algunos **instrumentos** se usan para observar.

V

vibrate (vī′ brāt) To move quickly back and forth. Drums make the air **vibrate.**

vibrar Moverse rápidamente hacia delante y hacia atrás. Los tambores hacen **vibrar** el aire.

volume (vol′ yəm) The amount of space matter takes up. You can use a measuring cup to measure the **volume** of liquids.

volumen Cantidad de espacio que ocupa la materia. Puedes usar una taza de medir para medir el **volumen** de un líquido.

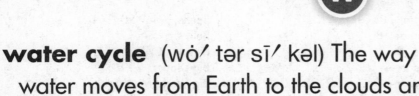

water cycle (wȯ′ tər sī′ kəl) The way water moves from Earth to the clouds and back to Earth again. Water condenses and evaporates in the **water cycle.**

ciclo del agua Manera en que se mueve el agua de la Tierra hacia las nubes y de nuevo a la Tierra. El agua se condensa y se evapora en el **ciclo del agua.**

wind (wind) Moving air. **Wind** can be very powerful.

viento Aire que se mueve. El **viento** puede ser muy fuerte.

Index

Page numbers for pictures, charts, graphs, maps, and their associated text are printed in *italic type*.

J

K

L

M

X rays, 43

Z

Credits

Staff Credits

The people who made up the *Interactive Science* team — representing composition services, core design digital and multimedia production services, digital product development, editorial, editorial services, manufacturing, and production — are listed below.

Geri Amani, Alisa Anderson, Jose Arrendondo, Amy Austin, David Bailis, Scott Baker, Lindsay Bellino, Charlie Bink, Bridget Binstock, Holly Blessen, Robin Bobo, Craig Bottomley, Jim Brady, Laura Brancky, Chris Budzisz, Odette Calderon, Mary Chingwa, Caroline Chung, Kier Cline, Brandon Cole, Mitch Coulter, AnnMarie Coyne, Fran Curran, Dana Damiano, Michael Di Maria, Nancy Duffner, Amanda Ferguson, David Gall, Mark Geyer, Amy Goodwin, Gerardine Griffin, Chris Haggerty, Margaret Hall, Laura Hancko, Autumn Hickenlooper, Guy Huff, George Jacobson, Marian Jones, Kathi Kalina, Chris Kammer, Sheila Kanitsch, Alyse Kondrat, Mary Kramer, Thea Limpus, Dominique Mariano, Lori McGuire, Melinda Medina, Angelina Mendez, Claudi Mimo, John Moore, Kevin Mork, Chris Niemyjski, Phoebe Novak, Anthony Nuccio, Jeff Osier, Charlene Rimsa, Rebecca Roberts, Camille Salerno, Manuel Sanchez, Carol Schmitz, Amanda Seldera, Jeannine Shelton El, Geri Shulman, Greg Sorenson, Samantha Sparkman, Mindy Spelius, Karen Stockwell, Dee Sunday, Dennis Tarwood, Jennie Teece, Lois Teesdale, Michaela Tudela, Karen Vuchichevich, Tom Wickland, James Yagelski, Tim Yetzina

Illustrations

104 Coleton Pyra; **106** Big Sesh Studios; **122, 143, 144, 145, 147, 148, 149, 153, 155, 159, 180, 210, 212, 227, 230, 238, 261, 284, 301, 316, EM11, EM12, EM22, EM24, EM27** Precision Graphics; **220, 231** Paul Oglesby; **220, 222, 227, EM22** Robert (Bob) Kayganich All other illustrations Chandler Digital Art

Photographs

Every effort has been made to secure permission and provide appropriate credit for photographic material. The publisher deeply regrets any omission and pledges to correct errors called to its attention in subsequent editions.

Unless otherwise acknowledged, all photographs are the property of Pearson Education, Inc.

Photo locators denoted as follows: Top (T), Center (C), Bottom (B), Left (L), Right (R), Background (Bkgd)

COVER: James Hager/Robert Harding Picture Library Ltd/Alamy

vi (TR) ©Getty Images/Jupiter Images; **vii** (TR) Getty Images; **viii** (TR) Digital Vision; **ix** (TR) ©Corbis/Jupiter Images; **x** (TR) ©Maslov Dmitry/Shutterstock; **xi** (TR) ©Wataru Yanagida/Getty Images; **xii** (TR) ©C. I. Aguera/Corbis; **xiii** (TR) ©David Trood/Getty Images; **xiv** (TR) ©keith morris/Alamy Images; **1** (Bkgrd) ©James Thew/Shutterstock, (Bkgrd) ©niderlander/Shutterstock;

2 (C) ©Purestock/Getty Images; **6** (T) ©Stocktrek RF/Getty Images, (B) JSC/NASA; **7** (CR) ©Hemis/Alamy Images; **8** (C) ©Michael Rosenfeld/Getty Images; **9** (CR) ©AFP/Getty Images, (CL) ©Jeff Greenberg/PhotoEdit, Inc.; **10** (T) ©zerega/Alamy; **11** (CR) ©Peter Dazeley/Getty Images; **12** (C) ©Photononstop/SuperStock; **14** (T) ©Getty Images/Jupiter Images; **15** (CR) Mary Clark; **19** (B) ©Anderson Ross/Getty Images; **20** (T) ©Gordon Wiltsie/Getty Images; **21** (CR) ©Getty Images/Jupiter Images; **24** (T) ©Andreas Scheler/Alamy; **25** (BR) James Osmond/Alamy Images; **26** (TR) Colin Keates/Courtesy of the Natural History Museum, London/©DK Images, (CR) DK Images; **30** (R) ©Jet Propulsion Laboratry/NASA Image Exchange, (TR) NASA; **31** (TC) ©Getty Images/Jupiter Images, (TR) ©Hemis/Alamy Images, (CR) ©Photononstop/SuperStock, (BC) James Osmond/Alamy Images, (BR) Mary Clark; **34** (BR) Jupiter Images; **35** (CR) ©Nigel Cattlin/Alamy Images; **36** (C) ©Jim Esposito Photography L. L. C./Getty Images; **39** (T) AlexMaster/Fotolia, (CC) ©Nando/Shutterstock; **40** (B) ©Bernd Mellmann/Alamy Images, (T) Getty Images; **41** (BR) ©Reuters/Corbis; **42** (BCR) ©JG Photography/Alamy, (BR) ©Roy Stevens/Time & Life Pictures/Getty Images, (BL) Dave King/Courtesy of The Science Museum, London/©DK Images, (CL) DK Images, (BCL) Simon Clay/Courtesy of the National Motor Museum, Beaulieu /©DK Images; **43** (TR) ©Paul Maguire/Shutterstock, (BL) Image Courtesy Eastman Kodak Company; **44** (T) ©Mike Flippo/Shutterstock; **45** (CR) ©Peter Gridley/Getty Images; **46** (TR) ©Paul Tearle/Thinkstock; **47** (BR) ©Denis and Yulia Pogostins/Shutterstock; **48** (Bkgrd) ©Evgeny Murtola/Shutterstock; **49** (BR) ©Blend Images/SuperStock; **50** (T) ©Emmanuel Lattes/Alamy Images; **51** (CR) ©Comstock/Thinkstock, (BL) Robert Cocquyt/Fotolia; **52** (TC) ©Massimiliano Leban/iStockphoto, (TR) ©Vstock/Alamy Stock Photo; **53** (CL) James R. Martin/Shutterstock, (TL) ©Comstock/Thinkstock, (CR) ©David Madison/Getty Images, (TR) ©Losevsky Pavel/Shutterstock, (BR) ©Mike Kemp/Getty Images; **54** (CR) ©Frank Cezus/Getty Images, (CL) ©Jason Kasumovic/Shutterstock, (CC) ©PhotoObjects/Thinkstock, (BL) Clive Streeter/©DK Images; **55** (CC) ©Brand X Pictures/Thinkstock, (BR) ©John E. Marriot/Getty Images, (BL) ©David Evison/Shutterstock, (CR) Peter Anderson/©DK Images; **58** (B) ©Arco Images GmbH/Alamy Images, (CR) Clint Keller/The Fort Wayne Journal/©AP Images; **59** (CC) ©Comstock/Thinkstock, (BR) ©Peter Gridley/Getty Images, (CR) ©Reuters/Corbis, (TR) Getty Images; **63** (TC) ©Massimiliano Leban/iStockphoto, (TR) Robert Cocquyt/Fotolia; **72** (Bkgrd) ©Clem Haagner/Photo Researchers, Inc., (L) ©Valueline/Punchstock; **75** (T) ©National Geographic Image Collection/Alamy; **76** (B) ©Digital Vision/Thinkstock, (TR, TC) ©Eric Isselée/Shutterstock; **77** (TL) ©Anat-oli/Shutterstock, (TL) ©Eric Isselée/Shutterstock, (CR) ©Leighton Photography & Imaging/Shutterstock, (TC) ©NIK/Shutterstock, (TR) ©Sascha Burkard/Shutterstock, (BR) ©Vinicius Tupinamba/Shutterstock; **78** (TR) ©Ian Scott/Shutterstock, (B) ©Shane Partridge/iStockphoto; **79** (CR) ©Cathy Keifer/Shutterstock, (BL) ©Eric Isselée/Shutterstock, (TC) ©Martin Pateman/Shutterstock; **80** (BL) ©Brett Stoltz/Shutterstock, (BR) Eric Isselée/Shutterstock; **81** (T) DK Images; **82** (T) Birdiegal/Fotolia; **83** (BR) Tania and Jim Thomson/123 RF; **84** (TR) ©Eric Gevaert/Shutterstock, (BR) ©Steve

Take Note

This space is yours. Draw pictures and write words.

interactive
SCIENCE

This is your book.

You can write in it.

This is your book.

You can write in it.

interactive SCIENCE

This is your book.

You can write in it.